CATALOGUE OF

✣ MEDIEVAL OBJECTS ✣

IN THE

MUSEUM OF FINE ARTS, BOSTON

Hanns Swarzenski   Nancy Netzer

· CATALOGUE OF MEDIEVAL OBJECTS ·

⚜ ENAMELS & GLASS ⚜

Hanns Swarzenski   Nancy Netzer

With a Technical Note by Pamela England

MUSEUM OF FINE ARTS

BOSTON

Library of Congress Catalogue Card Number 85-63531
ISBN 0-87846-263-5 (Cloth)
ISBN 0-87846-274-0 (Paper)

This publication is supported by a grant from the National
Endowment for the Arts, a Federal agency. The following
have also made generous contributions:
Claude Braillard
John Goelet
Edith I. Welch
John L. Gardner
John P. Axelrod

Typeset and printed by Acme Printing Co.,
Medford, Massachusetts

Designed by Carl Zahn

Photographic work comes from the MFA Department of
Photographic Services – Alan Newman and John Wolf –
with the exception of the following: Art Institute of Chicago (fig. 15); Metropolitan Museum of Art, New York
(figs. 18 and 21); Victoria and Albert Museum, London
(figs. 24 and 27); Kestner-Museum, Hanover (fig. 26);
Virginia Museum of Fine Arts, Richmond (figs. 17 and
20); Cluny Museum, Paris (figs. 22 and 23); Kunsthistorisches Museum, Vienna (fig. 25).

· PREFACE ·

In the fall of 1982 Hanns Swarzenski returned to Boston and to the department of European Decorative Arts and Sculpture for a visit of two months. It was the suggestion of Jan Fontein that we invite the department's distinguished curator emeritus, to help me and the members of my staff to know our collections and their history better. Hanns had in large part formed and guided the development of the department between 1948 and 1971, making many brilliant acquisitions in his special field of medieval art, as well as in the vast chronological span between the Renaissance and the mid-twentieth century. During his stay that fall and in two subsequent visits, he brought the collection alive in a new and wonderful way. Telling us many important things about its unwritten history – the patrons and collectors, dealers, and other personalities who had been the key figures in its formation – Hanns gave a sense of continuity to the department. With warmth, wit, and a prodigious memory combined with his extraordinary erudition, he would go through the galleries and storage areas with us, enlightening us about the objects in the collection. He spoke not only of their manufacture, historical significance, and particular aesthetic appeal but also of the way in which they had been acquired,

unraveling each marvelous story like a great mystery.

The desire to record Hanns's vast knowledge about each of the objects in the collection – and their relation to those in other collections – was the genesis of the present catalogue. His scholarship was complemented by the skills of Nancy Netzer, now a research fellow in the department, in research and writing. Their collaboration was a particularly happy and productive one.

Hanns enriched all of our lives personally and professionally, as Jan Fontein knew he would. I should like to thank the director for having first suggested that we invite Hanns to return to the Museum, and to thank Nancy Netzer for her splendid work as co-author of the catalogue. The contribution of Pamela England is greatly appreciated also; her technical and scientific analyses brought significant new information to the entries. Above all, I wish to express my gratitude to Hanns, whose greatness was evident in his kindness, his tolerance, and his endless enthusiasm for learning about and looking at works of art.

ANNE L. POULET
Russell B. and Andrée Beauchamp Stearns
Curator of European
Decorative Arts and Sculpture

· HANNS SWARZENSKI   1903 – 1985 ·

· A MEDIEVALIST & RENAISSANCE MAN ·

On June 22, 1985, Hanns Swarzenski died at Haus Hollerberg, Wilzhofen (Upper Bavaria), where he and his wife Brigitte had lived since his retirement from the Museum of Fine Arts in 1972. His death ended a long brilliant and fruitful career as a scholar, connoisseur, museum curator, and teacher. While his achievements were accomplished, and the influence of his vast knowledge was felt, on both sides of the Atlantic, it was the Museum of Fine Arts that was the principal institution to benefit from his inspiring presence and that became the permanent repository of most of his finest acquisitions.

Born in Berlin on August 30, 1903, Hanns followed in the footsteps of his father, Georg Swarzenski (1876-1957), and became a scholar of medieval art. In 1928, shortly after receiving his Ph.D. from the University of Bonn, where he studied under Paul Clemen, he came to Harvard University as a foreign scholar. It was his first encounter with the new world in which he would be destined to live and work for more than half of his entire life.

Returning to Berlin in 1929, he served as an assistant to Otto Kümmel in the preparations for the great Berlin exhibition of Chinese art. This was the swan song of the colorful German *côterie* of collectors of Chinese art, for only a few years later, with the rise of the Third Reich, the great exodus of scholars, collectors, and collections began. Hanns Swarzenski was soon to join in this greatest brain drain of all time, but before he emigrated to the United States in 1936 he worked at the Kunsthistorisches Institut in Florence, the Berlin State Museums, and the State Service for Monuments and Parks.

With a brief interruption during World War II, when he served as acting curator of sculpture at the National Gallery in Washington, D.C., he was active, from 1936 to 1948, as a research fellow at the Institute for Advanced Study at Princeton. Gifted with a creative ability to turn adversity into a positive force – he

loved to explain the motto *Palma sub pondere crescit* – the early years of exile were among his most productive. It was during this period that he completed several important articles as well as two seminal books, the *Berthold Missal* (1943) and *Monuments of Romanesque Art* (1954), brilliant studies that firmly established his scholarly credentials worldwide.

In 1948 he came to the Museum of Fine Arts as a fellow for research in the Department of Paintings, then led by W.G. Constable. Until 1952 he held this position concurrently with that of director of studies at the Warburg Institute in London. Between 1953 and 1972 he resided in the Museum's Department of European Decorative Arts and Sculpture, first as fellow for research and later as curator. The tangible results of Hanns Swarzenski's resourcefulness can be seen in both the Department of Paintings and the Department of Decorative Arts and Sculpture, where the presence of so many masterpieces can be attributed exclusively to his curatorial initiative. Their incredibly wide range from medieval to contemporary and their consistent artistic quality reveal the breadth of vision, the depth of knowledge, and the keen eye of a true renaissance man. His friendship with collectors and art dealers on both sides of the Atlantic made his annual summer forays to Europe in the company of Perry Rathbone and his frequent excursions to the New York art market adventures of discovery. Thus, with the unfailing support of trustees and director, both he and his father helped to bring together one of the last great collections of medieval art.

The Museum is fortunate to have benefited from his knowledge of the arts until the very end of his life. To his younger colleagues, with whom he invariably maintained the most cordial relations, he set a rare example of thorough scholarship, impeccable connoisseurship, and, above all, moral integrity and breadth of vision. All who had the privilege of working with him can only be grateful for the good fortune that brought them together with this great man, who will always be fondly remembered and whose absence will be keenly felt in the years to come. A few weeks before his death he reviewed the manuscript of this catalogue, retaining until his last days the passionate dedication to and infectious enthusiasm for works of art that had characterized his entire life. We hope that in the final editing and production of the catalogue we have been able to do justice to the high standards he strove to maintain and to the high expectations he cherished. May this catalogue serve as a lasting monument to his scholarship and be worthy of the exquisite objects that he acquired with unfailing devotion, discernment, and zest for life.

JAN FONTEIN
Director

· CONTENTS ·

· ACKNOWLEDGMENTS ·

In the process of writing this catalogue we have been aided by many people, whom I should like to thank here. The director of the Museum, Jan Fontein, had the initial idea for this project and supported it in numerous ways over the past three years. Anne L. Poulet, the curator of European Decorative Arts and Sculpture, proposed the undertaking and raised the necessary funds for its completion. It is to her that we owe our greatest debt of gratitude. Truly, she has made our work as pleasant as possible, supervising the project at every stage and making many suggestions for the organization and phrasing of the text. Without her the catalogue would not exist.

Much of the information in the detailed descriptions of the objects was provided by research scientists on the staff, Pamela England and Lambertus van Zelst (now of the Smithsonian Institution in Washington). They undertook the task of examining and analyzing the components of each object with great enthusiasm and often graciously corrected a number of this art historian's misconceptions about technique. The many hours of collaboration with them could not have been more rewarding or more enriching.

Ellen Berkman, my indefatigable research assistant for two summers, measured the objects and compiled much of the bibliography and information on provenance for this volume and for subsequent publication. The consistency with which this material is presented is, in large part, the result of her precision and care. Caroline Guion, a student intern, checked the bibliographic references.

Our friends and colleagues in the Department of European Decorative Arts and Sculpture, Ellenor Alcorn, Diana Larsen, Michele Marincola, Cathy Modica, and Jeffrey Munger, have been a source of unfailing encouragement and good humor. For them thanks are most inadequate; they listened patiently to ideas in their incipient stages and offered much helpful criticism. In addition, Michele cleaned a number of the objects before they were photographed, and Ellenor supervised the photography of several objects with a most discriminating eye.

The photography was efficiently coordinated by Janice Sorkow, director of the Museum's Photo Services Department, who seemed always to understand our needs. Alan Newman and John Woolf succeeded in creating images that accurately reveal the shape and decoration of the objects. We thank also Thomas Lang, who printed the photographs, and Ann Petrone and Joellen Secondo, who catalogued them.

The research has been aided greatly by the librarian, Nancy Allen, and her staff. Bonnie Porter secured on interlibrary loan even the most obscure articles and books and, understanding the pressures of our deadline, Eve Morgan and Laila Abdel-Malek ordered and catalogued new publications with great efficiency.

The task of editing the manuscript fell to Judy Spear, whom I am pleased to acknowledge. She read the text with extraordinary discernment, and it should be said that the book has benefited in no small way from her talents. Carl Zahn, the Museum's Director of Publications, has helped with the planning from the very beginning. He is responsible for the sensitive and beautiful design of the book and for supervising its printing.

In the course of our research, we have been helped by several scholars. Dietrich Kötzsche of the Kunstgewerbemuseum in Berlin was infinitely generous with his knowledge of Mosan and Rhenish enamels and in sharing his ideas on the pieces included here. Also greatly beneficial were the observations of Charles Little and Renate Eikelmann of the Metropolitan Museum in New York, who, on separate occasions, visited Boston and reviewed the objects. They have been most hospitable on our trips to the Metropolitan and responded to endless requests for information on objects there. Many of the comparative pieces cited in the entries on the Limoges enamels were found in the archive of Marie-Madeleine Gauthier in Paris, who welcomed me in her home and granted me access to her comprehensive files. She and her assistant, Geneviève François, answered questions and made many helpful suggestions for the entries.

Numerous colleagues in this museum and others, scholars, dealers, and collectors have assisted in various ways and have shown us objects in their collections. We want to thank: Peter Barnet, Detroit Institute of Arts; Robert Bergman, Walters Art Gallery, Baltimore; Roger Berkowitz, Toledo Museum of Art; Mavis Bimson, British Museum, London; Martin Blindheim, University Museum of National Antiquities, Oslo; Ruth Blumka, New York; Barbara Boehm, Metropolitan Museum of Art, New York; D'A.J. Boulton, South Bend, Indiana; Susan Boyd, Dumbarton Oaks, Washington, D.C.; Michael Brandt, Diözesanmuseum, Hildesheim; Harry Brooks, Wildenstein and Co., New York; Katharine Brown, Metropolitan Museum of Art; Ella Brummer, New York; David Buckton, British Museum; Tord Buggeland, De Sandvigske Samlinger-Maihaugen, Lillehammer, Sweden; David H. Caldwell, National Museum of Antiquities of Scotland, Edinburgh; Richard Camber, Sotheby & Co., London; Marian Campbell, Victoria and Albert Museum, London; Madeline Caviness, Tufts University, Medford, Massachusetts; Elizabeth Delahaye, Musée de Cluny, Paris; Cara Denison, Pierpont Morgan Library, New York; Deborah Dluhy, Museum of Fine Arts, Boston; Jannic Durand, Musée du Louvre, Paris; Wolfgang Eckhardt, Museum für Kunst und Gewerbe, Hamburg; Danielle Gaborit, Musée du Louvre, Paris; Margaret Gibson, University of Liverpool; Dorothy Gillerman, Boston; Catherine Gras, Musée des Beaux-Arts, Dijon; John Herrmann, Museum of Fine Arts, Boston; Helga Hilschenz-Mylneck, Kestner Museum, Hanover; Gertrude Hunt, Dublin; Timothy Husband, Metropolitan Museum of Art; Ernst Kitzinger, Oxford, England; Ellen Kosmer, Worcester State College; Thomas Kren, J. Paul Getty Museum, Malibu; Marta Kryshanovskaja, The State Hermitage, Leningrad; Jacqueline Lafontaine-Dosogne, Musée Cinquantenaire, Brussels; Anton Legner, Schnütgen-Museum, Cologne; Albert Lemeunier, Musée d'art religieusxe et d'art mosan, Liège; Niels-Knud Liebgott, Nationalmuseet, Copenhagen; Meredith Lillich, Syracuse University; Sonia Lismer, Allen Memorial Art Museum, Oberlin, Ohio; Edward R. Lubin, New York; Giovanni Morello, Museo Sacro, Vatican; Florentine Mütherich, Zentralinstitut für Kunstgeschichte, Munich; Pinkney Near, Virginia Museum of Fine Arts, Richmond; Karel Otavsky, Abegg-Stiftung, Riggisberg; Richard Randall, Baltimore, Maryland; William Robinson, Pierpont Morgan Library, New York; Betsy Rosasco, The Art Museum, Princeton University; Michael Ryan, National Museum of Ireland, Dublin; Willibald Sauerländer, Zentralinstitut für Kunstgeschichte, Munich; Stephen Scher, Kinnelon, New Jersey; Walter Schulten, Domschatz, Cologne; Kathleen Scott, Ann Arbor, Michigan; Annie Scottez, Musée des Beaux-Arts, Lille; Nancy Sevcenko, Cambridge, Massachusetts; Marilyn Stokstad, University of Kansas, Lawrence; Neil Stratford, British Museum; Göran Tegnér, Statens Historiska Museum, Stockholm; Anne van Buren, Tufts University; Mary Jane Victor, Menil Foundation, Inc., Houston; Gary Vikan, Walters Art Gallery; William Voekle, Pierpont Morgan Library; Hildegard Vogeler, Bayerisches Nationalmuseum, Munich; Karen Weiss, Archives of American Art, Washington, D.C.; Roger Wieck, Walters Art Gallery; Paul Williamson, Victoria and Albert Museum; Patrick de Winter, Cleveland Museum of Art; William Wixom, Metropolitan Museum of Art; Rainer Zietz, London; George Zarnecki, Courtauld Institute of Art, London.

A particular expression of gratitude is due the National Endowment for the Arts, which contributed generously to both the research and the publication of the present catalogue. The Museum's grant officer, Janet Spitz, aided us with painstaking care in preparing the applications and the budgets that went into them.

Especially in days when sufficient funds for a scholarly undertaking such as this are so hard to come by, we were fortunate to have the aid of several individuals. Were it not for John Goelet, an old friend of Hanns Swarzenski's and the department, who supported the early planning and research for the catalogue both here and abroad, we would not have been able to apply for our first NEA grant. Edith Welch made it possible for me to work before the NEA grant began; John L. Gardner underwrote my first research trip abroad; Claude Braillard, with John Axelrod, supplied the funds necessary to see the manuscript through publication; she also underwrote the cost of the color reproductions. To each of them, I extend heartfelt thanks, for without them, this project would not have gone forward.

In conclusion, I should like to thank my husband, Bob, and Hanns, I know, would want to thank his wife, Brigitte. What the catalogue owes to their support can never be acknowledged adequately.

Finally, I wish to thank Hanns, who introduced me to these objects and taught me to love and to understand them. Even in his absence, he remains the best of collaborators; his ideas and inspiration will always be with me.

N.N.

The third largest collection of medieval art in this country after those of the Walters Art Gallery in Baltimore and the Metropolitan Museum in New York, Boston's began not through private donations but through the agency of two great curators. Between 1939 and 1971, Georg Swarzenski and his son Hanns, both distinguished scholars and connoisseurs in the field, assembled for the Museum approximately three hundred fifty objects from the middle ages.

Forced to leave his country and his position of more than thirty years as director of the Städel Art Institute and Municipal Gallery in Frankfurt-am-Main, Georg Swarzenski came to Boston in 1939. He had been one of the leaders not only in the museum world but in the intellectual life of Germany in the pre-Nazi period, and his prominent role in the art historical community was to continue after his emigration to America. Following his arrival in Boston, he organized for the MFA one of this country's first loan exhibitions of medieval art – "Arts of the Middle Ages 1000-1400." At the same time, taking advantage of the quantity of objects from private European sources that had recently become available as a result of political circumstances, he began to build the Museum's collection. A founder of Frankfurt's Liebieghaus Museum, Georg Swarzenski had been instrumental in assembling there outstanding works thought to be characteristic of the development of sculpture; he and his son sought to do much the same for Boston.

Acknowledged as the most gifted connoisseur of medieval art of his generation, Hanns Swarzenski had already made significant contributions to the building of the Museum's collections before he arrived in 1948. While at the Institute for Advanced Study in Princeton between 1936 and 1948, he had located many of the objects purchased for the Museum by his father. After the war and before his retirement as curator of European decorative arts

and sculpture in 1971 – acquainted with every dealer, private collector and provincial museum with medieval art – Hanns traveled extensively in Europe, where he discovered most of the pieces in the collection today. His *Monuments of Romanesque Art* demonstrated that the so-called minor arts, or *kleinkunst*, of the middle ages were more major than minor in conception and importance; thus, it should come as no surprise that two thirds of the objects he brought to Boston are small in scale.

Although this catalogue of sixty medieval enamels and glass objects presents only a small portion of the collection assembled by the Swarzenskis, it nonetheless epitomizes several of their scholarly interests. It is not without significance that out of the nine glass objects three (nos. 51, 52, and 53) are Italian gilded glass of the Gothic period. Georg Swarzenski was one of the first to study this glass as a group and made important contributions to the literature on it. Two of the three examples were formerly in his own collection; the third was purchased on the advice of Hanns by an enthusiastic supporter of the collection, John Goelet, who later gave it to the Museum.

That the enamels are far more numerous, and that they are primarily of European rather than Eastern Mediterranean origin, may also be attributed more to the specific interests of the Swarzenskis than to the availability of the objects when they were acquired. The large group of Mosan and Rhenish enamels is explainable in part by Hanns's tenure as a student of Paul Clemen, the great cataloguer of the artistic monuments of the Rhineland, through whom he came to know the objects from this area intimately. Hanns's first job as a graduate student was to assist in the preparation of the *Jahrtausendaustellung* in Düsseldorf in 1925, where all of the great Rhenish treasures were displayed; his dissertation (1927) and book, *Die lateinischen illuminierten Handschriften des XIII Jahrhunderts in den Ländern an Rhein, Main und Donau* (1936), remain un-

Hanns and Georg Swarzenski at the Hearst Sale in 1941

surpassed as basic studies on the Romanesque and Gothic manuscripts from this region.

The Swarzenskis sought to acquire objects of rarity and unusual quality rather than to form a systematically complete collection. Each of the principal medieval enameling techniques – *cloisonné*, champlevé, *basse-taille*, and painted – has here at least one example; however, the collection is by no means representative of the history of enamel work in the middle ages. From the early period, there is a single example, the superb Emly Shrine (no. 1), and examples from two large and important groups, Byzantine *cloisonné* and Italian *basse-taille* enamels, are lacking altogether. The modus operandi for acquiring exceptional pieces is perhaps best illustrated by the examples Hanns and his father chose from the large

corpus of Limoges objects. A Baptism of extraordinary quality (no. 32) was certainly conceived as a unique object; a small box divided into two compartments on the inside (no. 27), an openwork pendant (no. 22), a mirror case (no. 33), and a round container showing a couple feasting (no. 35) are types with very few parallels among Limoges objects; a eucharistic dove (no. 26) is unique among the forty known examples of its type in having its receptacle under the wing; and a Crucifix (no. 23) belongs to a rare group showing the figure crowned and clothed.

Among the objects in the present catalogue, only four were in the collection prior to Georg Swarzenski's arrival. A Limoges plaque with a standing Christ (no. 25) had been given in 1885 by Alfred Greenough, the brother of the sculptor Horatio Greenough and one of the few American collectors of medieval objects in the nineteenth century; a Limoges pyx (no. 28) was a gift of Horatio Curtis in 1915; a large stained-glass window from Hampton court (no. 54) was purchased in London in 1925 for installation in the Museum's new decorative arts wing; and a *cloisonné* medallion with Saint Nicholas (no. A1) was bought from a dealer in New York in 1928. The Swarzenskis purchased nearly all of the rest, the largest group of which passed through the hands of the New York dealer Joseph Brummer. Eight enamels (nos. 2, 7, 23, 33, 37, 41, 42, and A6) – as well as many medieval objects in other media – were bought at the famous Brummer sale in 1949. The trustees had appropriated a fixed sum to be spent at the discretion of the Swarzenskis, who attended the sale together. Ten enamels (nos. 6, 8, 9, 13, 14, 15, 17, 20, 45, and A3) had been purchased from Brummer on separate occasions a few years before the sale. Four of these (nos. 13, 14, 15, and 17), *spolia* from large shrines in Cologne and Siegburg, are said to have been bought by Brummer from a Paris dealer who, in turn, purchased them from Paul Beumers, a Düsseldorf jeweler who restored a number of Rhenish shrines around the turn of the century. Beumers imitated the enamels of the shrines he restored so perfectly that his replacements are often difficult to distinguish from the originals. He not only sold reproductions, but he is said to have substituted his own pieces for originals on the shrine, which he later sold.

Among other well-known dealers in medieval art from whom works in this volume were purchased are John Hunt in Dublin (nos. 18, 22, and 39) and several in New York: Rosenberg and Stiebel (nos. 9, 36, 38, and 43), Leopold Blumka (nos. 24, 27, and 46), Georges Wildenstein (nos. 5, 32, and 52), Mathias Komor (no. 44), and Raphael Stora

(nos. 10, 21, and 26). Some of the pieces were given to the Museum by dealers (nos. 18, 22, 27, and 46), and several were known to the Swarzenskis, before they appeared on the art market in America, from private European collections. Georg had advised several prominent Frankfurt collectors and thus knew well the splendid painted spoon (no. 43), the triptych reliquary (no. 38), and the Limoges plaques with beasts (no. 36) from the collection of Max von Goldschmidt-Rothschild, as well as the Lower Saxon plaque with Apostles (no. 21) and the long plaque (no. 10) that had belonged first to R. von Gontard-Passavant and then to Harry Fuld. In 1959, Hanns purchased from Otto Wertheimer in Paris a fine gold brooch (no. 47) that he had admired for many years in the collection of Marc Rosenberg, the well-known scholar of metalwork whom he often visited in Baden-Baden during his student days.

Several of the objects belonged to important collectors of enamels in the nineteenth century: Spitzer (no. A3), Germeau (nos. 32 and 37), Czartoryski (nos. 5 and 32), and Eumorphopoulos (no. 33). The casket with beasts in scrolls (no. 3), thought to be Mosan until Hanns bought it from a Paris dealer and established its origin as English, was in both the DeBruge-Dumenil and Soltykoff collections. Two significant collections of enamels in the twentieth century represented here are those of D. Schevitch (no. 41) and Phillip Nelson (no. 4).

The genius of Georg and Hanns Swarzenski in gathering this outstanding group of enamels with distinguished provenance without the advantage of lavish purchase funds cannot be overestimated. They had a rare talent for finding objects and for singling out the exceptional among them. Drawing on their years of experience in the field, they created for Boston one of the finest monuments to medieval art.

N.N.

Fig. 4. X-ray radiography can reveal tool marks, especially those of the chisel, beneath areas of intact enamel. An interesting variant on the common chiseling technique is illustrated in this radiograph of the front side of an English casket (see no. 3). Here a few "islands" of copper were raised from the base of the fields using a fine chisel. This further ensured that the enamel was attached to the copper. The same phenomenon can be observed on a well-known group of three English ciboria[4] and on some enamels from Lower Saxony.

Fig. 5. An x-radiograph detail shows radial tool marks beneath the enamel of the halo and details of the engraving (see no. 6). There is a dark line delineating the main design elements, corresponding to a deeper engraved line in the copper plaque. The study of these engraving lines revealed by x-radiography enables a comparison between the styles of different schools of enamelers.[5]

Fig. 8. An x-radiograph of a eucharistic dove of the Limoges School (see no. 26) shows the technique of construction. The glass eyes conceal the two ends of a pin, one of many joining the two halves of the body. The beak is one end of a piece of metal (gilded brass) that extends through the hollow head and ends on the outside at the back. The radiograph also shows that the tail is repaired with modern solder (see the light area of the radiograph).

· A TECHNICAL INVESTIGATION ·
OF MEDIEVAL ENAMELS

TECHNIQUES OF ENAMELING

Enamel is a vitreous material that is applied to a metal support in powdered form and held in position by its subsequent fusion and bonding with the metal. During the medieval period, powdered enamel was produced in glass workshops; therefore, a discussion of the starting materials, colorants, and opacifiers of enamels is inseparable from that of contemporary glass. The technique of enameling should not be confused with that of inlaid cut glass or unfused glass paste pressed into a prepared metal base.

Among the objects described in this catalogue four enameling methods are represented. The earliest is *cloisonné*, in which thin metallic bands or wires are shaped into a design and soldered to a metal base plate. The fields are then filled with powdered enamel and fired. When translucent enamels are applied to the metal – usually gold – the reflection of light from the metal through the enamel imparts a brilliant gem-like quality to the piece. Indeed, this technique is believed to have evolved in imitation of the more costly practice of applying gems and semiprecious stones in a *cloisonné* framework. During the eleventh century, *cloisonné* enamel work in western Europe gradually declined. Because of the expense and scarcity of gold at this time, enamels were made with a copper support and subsequently gilded in imitation of gold.

In *champlevé* enameling, a technique that reached its peak in the twelfth century, the design is chiseled out of a copper plaque and the cells thus formed are filled with powdered enamel and fired. Fusion of the enamel results in a thin reaction layer of red copper oxide at the metal-enamel interface; this can be seen in damaged areas and around the edges of the color fields (see fig. 1). The reaction, which helps to bond the enamel to the copper, has the undesirable effect of altering the color of translucent enamel. Consequently, the colors used in *champlevé* enamels on copper are, for the most part, semitranslucent or opaque. On occasion, a thin gold foil, covered with translucent enamel, is found at the base of a *champlevé* field.[1]

In *basse-taille* enameling (see fig. 2), the design is outlined in silver and surface details are delineated by chasing and engraving in low relief. Variations in the thickness of enamel applied over the silver support create subtle modelings of light and shade. With the exception of an opaque red, the enamels of *basse-taille* are transparent; they are often modified by placing gold foil on selected parts of the design before the powdered enamel is put in position.

Powdered enamels, mixed with a gum binder, can also be painted onto a metal support (see no. 43), usually copper or silver. An opaque white serves as an underlayer for the translucent enamels applied subsequently.

While much of our understanding of the technique derives from microscopic observation, we are also indebted to the writings of the monk Theophilus, who is generally believed to have worked as a metalsmith in a twelfth-century German abbey. His treatise, *De Diversis Artibus*, provides an invaluable insight into the manufacture of glass and the preparation of enamels.[2] Theophilus emphasized the importance of removing impurities from the copper before it was formed into *champlevé* baseplates. The purification was most important if the craftsman intended to gild the finished piece: ". . . if you see white spots emerging . . . this is the fault of the . . . lead, because the copper was not purged and refined free of it" (Book 3, Chapter 68). Since they form an amalgam with gold and cause blistering of the gold surface when they are volatilized during the heating stage, both lead and zinc interfere with the formation of a smooth gold surface. In addition, the presence of small amounts of zinc can affect the bonding between the metal and the enamel.

Theophilus advised that copper be subjected to testing by hammering in order to evaluate the success of the refining process: ". . .if it breaks or splits, it will have to be melted again in the same way" (Book 3, Chapter 67).[3] Once purified, the copper is hammered into plaques between 2 and 5 millimeters thick that are either flat or shaped around a wooden form. The design is then engraved onto the copper and metal is chiseled out of the fields to a depth of 0.5 to 1 millimeter (see figs. 3, 4, and 5).

Theophilus recommended that the melting ranges of the enamels first be determined by placing them on a copper sheet and fusing them simultaneously in an oven (Book 3, Chapter 54). Although these instructions might suggest a single fusion of the various colors, this is not necessarily the case. For example, white is relatively stable and would remain unchanged by repeated firings.[5] The powdered enamel is placed in the sunken areas (see fig. 6), and is fired on an iron tray covered with a perforated lid and surrounded by charcoal.[6] The surface of the object is then ground so that the enamel is flush with the reserved areas of copper (see fig. 7). Finally, the surface is polished and gilded.

In the process of gilding, mercury and gold are ground together to form a paste. The amalgam is applied to the copper and heated so that the mercury is driven off as a vapor, leaving a continuous layer of gold. Finally, the gilded surface is burnished to bring the gold to a high degree of finish. The completed enamel plaques are then assembled, forming either small decorative works such as boxes that are soldered, pinned, or hinged, or more elaborate objects such as shrines consisting of a large wooden framework to which the components are nailed (see fig. 8).

THE COMPOSITION OF MEDIEVAL GLASS AND ENAMEL

The primary analytical technique used in this investigation is energy-dispersive x-ray fluorescence spectrometry – a nondestructive method of analysis.[7] The technique has a major drawback when used to analyze glassy materials; as a rule, it cannot detect the presence of elements below calcium in the periodic table. This means that none of the major components of the glass matrix – silicon, sodium, and potassium – can be determined. Therefore, the classification of the glass as soda-lime ("Roman") or potash ("medieval northern European") is not possible. However, the method does permit the identification

of the coloring and opacifying agents, which contain elements heavier than calcium.

Glass and enamel are composed of quartz sand and an alkali (sodium or potassium) salt as a fluxing agent. Lime is also present in ancient glass but, as there is no specific mention of this in recipes until the sixteenth century,[8] it was probably introduced as an impurity along with other components. Nevertheless, its presence is beneficial because the calcium it contains stabilizes the glass matrix, making it less susceptible to degradation and attack by hygroscopic salts.

Roman glasses have a soda-lime composition that is remarkably consistent throughout the area of the empire, suggesting that glass fabrication was standardized. Since there was no readily available source of soda in northern Europe, the Romans probably imported it to their provincial glassworks from the Mediterranean area. With the fall of the Roman Empire in the West, supplies of soda dwindled and alternative sources of alkali had to be found, especially with a growing demand for window glass for the cathedrals of medieval Europe. As early as the ninth century, wood ash (potash) came to be exploited for its potassium content, and glass workshops moved from town sites into the forests to be closer to the supplies of ash.[9]

In even the purest starting materials, other components, such as calcium (a necessary contaminant), iron, aluminum, and magnesium, are present. Theophilus urged the glassmaker to select only the purest washed river sand and to exercise great care when preparing the wood ash to ensure that no trace of soil was included (Book 2, Chapter 4). Despite these precautions, there was usually sufficient iron present to impart a pale greenish tinge to the glass. Before the medieval period, antimony or manganese salts were added to oxidize the iron and thus counter this undesirable effect.[10] However, if one follows the account in *On Divers Arts* (Book 2, Chapters 5-8), describing the preparation of window glass, it is not at all clear that the complex manipulation of the number of variables involved in decolorizing the glass was controlled during the medieval period.[11] The presence of manganese in wood ash, usually prepared from beech or oak trees, as well as the variable amounts of iron impurity being introduced, meant that the starting materials were far from constant. Excessive amounts of manganese over iron produce a pale pink or purple coloration; in addition, irreproducible atmospheric conditions within the furnace and varying times of heating all tended to introduce a certain unpredictability into the process.[12]

Lead can also be a constituent of a vitreous matrix and, when present, modifies its physical properties by increasing the fluidity of the semimolten material and lowering its surface tension; both of these modifications are advantageous when a piece of *champlevé* enamel is being fired because they result in a more complete filling of the fields. Lead influences the color of a copper glass or enamel and improves the solubility of copper and antimony.[13] In the presence of elements such as tin and antimony, lead reacts to form opaque yellow colorants.

Coloring and Opacifying Agents

Glasses and enamels are usually colored and opacified by the addition of small amounts of metallic elements. During the medieval period, the coloring and opacifying agents were incorporated as metals or ores. The colors obtained could be modified by the oxidizing or reducing conditions prevailing in the furnace, the time of heating, the nature of the alkali in the glass (sodium or potassium), and the presence of lead. The variety of colors of powdered glass available to the medieval enameler, although somewhat limited, could be expanded by mixing them before firing, provided that their melting ranges were compatible[14] (see fig. 9).

Blue, Red, Green, and Purple

The lapis blue found on many enamels results from the addition of a small amount of a cobalt ore. Quantities as low as 0.2 percent of cobalt are sufficient to produce a deep blue. Copper is also a component of this blue, although its presence does not seem to affect the color.[13] In many of the deep blues analyzed on enamels attributed to the Limoges school, zinc is detectable; this is not the case for any of the Mosan lapis blues. Whether the zinc derives from the source of the cobalt, or is a contaminant from brass crucibles used in the glass formulation, is unclear.

Copper is responsible for a range of colors – blue, turquoise, green, and red – depending on the other components of the matrix, especially the alkali.[1,13,15] Where the alkali is sodium, the color tends to be a turquoise blue. This was confirmed by the electron microprobe analysis of a chip of turquoise enamel removed from a colonnette (no. 16). Copper in a glass containing potassium, however, yields a green.

Opaque copper-red enamel derives from minute crystals of copper or of red copper oxide suspended in the glass matrix and, thereby, opacifying it. Red is the final color to be applied to the enamel as it is liable to become oxidized (see fig. 10).[16]

The transparent green of three of the *basse-taille* enamels (nos. 39, 40, and 41) is colored by chromium (see fig. 2), which is not considered to have been used until the early nineteenth century. As long as there are no analyses of similar material available for comparison, the discovery of chromium in medieval pieces must be considered suspect.[17]

Manganese renders the glass purple. However, it may not have been added intentionally in the medieval period; there may have been sufficient manganese present in the potash to induce a purple coloration. In this group of *champlevé* enamels, the only example of manganese purple is found on the decoration of the lid of an English casket (no. 3; see fig. 11). Another contemporary example has a layer of opaque white beneath the purple, presumably designed to enhance the color.[4]

Yellow

The identity of opaque yellow glass colorants has received a great deal of attention.[18] In antiquity, crystals of yellow lead antimonate, which are suspended in the glass, colored it and rendered it opaque. During the fourth and fifth centuries A.D., the opaque yellow colorant of glass changed to a mixed lead-tin oxide.[18,19] Somewhat surprisingly, lead-tin-oxide yellow is encountered on only one of the pieces examined in this survey – the late-seventh- to early-eighth-century Irish shrine (no. 1; see fig. 12); the yellow usually found is lead antimonate.[1,15,20] Its unexpected presence during the medieval period in Europe, when antimony was thought to be unknown, is explained by reference to a passage by Theophilus: "Different kinds of glass, namely, white, black, green, yellow, blue and purple, are found in mosaic work in ancient buildings. These are not transparent but are opaque like marble, like little square stones, and enamel work is made from them . . ." (Book 2, Chapter 12).

The text has been interpreted to mean that mosaic tesserae were being excavated from Roman buildings and reused by medieval artisans.[21] Furthermore, evidence from analysis of the opaque yellows of these enamels tends to confirm the reuse of Roman materials, as implied by Theophilus. In this collection of enamels, there are more instances of yellow in the Mosan pieces than in the examples from the later Limoges school. This might indicate that the supply of Roman tesserae was diminishing by the beginning of the thirteenth century.

Analysis of an enamel attributed to the late-eleventh-century Conques School in central southern France (no. 2) raises an interesting question. The yellow enamel on the halo is colored by uranium, which was used as a glass colorant in the nineteenth century[22] (see fig. 13).

White Enamels and Opacifiers

The history of the use of opaque white glass is well documented and is similar to that of opaque yellow.[18] In antiquity, it was formed by the reaction between lime and an antimony ore, yielding calcium antimonate. From approximately A.D. 300, the use of calcium-antimonate opacifiers declined in favor of tin oxide. There is a formulation for an opaque tin-containing glass in the *Mappae Clavicula* (Chapter 56) in a section that derives from a ninth-century manuscript: "Making glass a milky colour: put 3 oz. of tin to a pound of glass and cook it for 2 days."[23]

However, the white enamels examined in this and other studies do not present such a straightforward picture.[1,15,20] The whites of the Mosan pieces contain antimony, probably as calcium antimonate; antimony is present also in other colors that are modified by white. This, again, lends credence to the passage in Theophilus quoted above, wherein the reuse of Roman tesserae is implied. The situation is different in consideration of the pieces of the Limoges school. Here the whites contain tin oxide.[24] (The yellows, however, are colored with lead antimonate.) Enamels attributed to the Cologne school seem to occupy a transitional place between the Mosan and later Limoges pieces; some have antimony in their whites and others contain tin oxide.[25]

In addition to the above-mentioned presence of zinc in the cobalt blues of Limoges enamels, the presence of a calcium-antimonate opacifier in pieces from the Mosan enamel workshops, and of a tin-oxide opacifier in those of the Limoges area, provides an important criterion in the attribution of medieval enamels. Continued confirmation of these observations might clarify uncertain attributions to the Mosan and Limoges schools of enamelers and also help to assess the influences of these two great centers on more provincial workshops.[26]

P.E.

REFERENCES AND FOOTNOTES

1. C. Lahanier, "Etude scientifique de la plaque émaillée de Geoffroy Plantagenet," *Annales du laboratoire de recherche des musées de France* (1982), pp. 7-28.

2. Theophilus, *"On Divers Arts,"* translated by C.S. Smith and J.G. Hawthorne (New York, 1979).

3. Analysis of a number of the plaques by x-ray fluorescence spectrometry indicates that copper is present in the range of 99 to 99.75 percent, with lead being the impurity evident at highest levels. While this amount of lead might interfere with the process of mercury gilding, it would also tend to make the copper easier to work.

4. G. Zarnecki, J. Holt, and T. Holland, eds., *English Romanesque Art 1066-1200* (London: Arts Council of Great Britain, 1984), nos. 278, 279, and 280.

5. N. Stratford, "The Henry of Blois Plaques in the British Museum," *Medieval Art and Architecture in Winchester* (British Archaeological Association, 1983), pp. 28-34.

6. In some pieces, red enamel appears to have been applied thinly over color previously fused and then the piece was subjected to another short firing (see fig. 6).

7. X-ray fluorescence spectrometry uses a narrow beam of x-rays to excite the constituent elements of the area being analyzed so that the electrons within the atoms are raised to a higher energy level. When the electrons return to their ground state – almost instantaneously – secondary x-rays are emitted with energies and wavelengths specific to the elements present. By detecting the x-rays and sorting them by energy (or wavelength), the spectrometer presents a qualitative determination of some of the elements. The size of the signal is proportional to the amounts of each element and, therefore, a semi-quantitative analysis is also possible.

Although the beam of x-rays is collimated to provide the analysis of an area approximately 2 to 3 millimeters in diameter, the data resulting from complex mixed color fields were treated with circumspection.

8. V. Biringuccio, *De la Pirotechnia*, translated by C.S. Smith and M.T. Gnudi (New York, 1942; originally published in Venice in 1540).

9. D. Buckton, "Necessity, the 'Mother of Invention' in Early Medieval Enamels," *Trans. Canadian Conf. of Med. Art Historians*, no. 3 (1982), (London [Ontario], 1985), pp. 1-6.

10. E.V. Sayre, "The Intentional Use of Antimony and Manganese in Ancient Glasses," *Advances in Glass Technology*, part 2, F.R. Matson and G.E. Rindane, eds. (New York, 1963), pp. 263-282.

11. R.G. Newton, "Colouring Agents Used by Medieval Glassmakers," *Glass Technology* 19, no. 3 (1978), pp. 59-60.

12. For a thorough discussion of this, the reader is referred to the footnotes in the Smith and Hawthorne translation of *On Divers Arts*, pp. 55-56 (see note 2).

13. L. Biek and L. Bayley, "Glass and Other Vitreous Materials," *World Archaeology* 11 (1979), pp. 1-25.

14. The evidence for the mixing of two or more powdered enamels is best obtained by the microscopic examination of the surface, rather than by interpreting the results of the chemical analysis.

15. M. Bimson, "A Preliminary Survey of Two Groups of Twelfth-Century Mosan Enamels," *Annales du 8ᵉ congrès international d'étude historique du verre* (Liège, 1981), pp. 161-164.

16. Microscopic examination shows that the red enamel was applied mixed with a clear lead glass (see fig. 10). The lead glass fuses at a lower temperature than the red enamel and melts, securing it in place and providing a measure of protection against oxidation during firing.

17. The amount of chromium found in the green suggests that it is not present as a contaminant but that it was being used purposefully as a colorant.

Chromium is also detectable in the green of a late-nineteenth-century *cloisonné* enamel on gold (no. A1), a *hanap* (no. A2), a pendant (no. A3), a plaque (no. A5), and a clasp (no. A6).

18. H.P. Rooksby, "Opacifiers in Opal Glasses," *G.E.C. Journal* 29, no. 1 (1962), pp. 20-26.

19. H. Kühn, "Lead-Tin Yellow," *Studies in Conservation* 13 (1968), pp. 7-33.

20. D. Buckton, "Enamelling on Gold," *Gold Bulletin* 15, no. 3 (1982), pp. 101-109.

21. It is surprising, however, that there was no trade in opaque lead-tin-oxide yellow glass from the eastern Mediterranean, where it was widely used. It would be interesting to compare yellow tesserae of the Roman period with those produced later in Byzantine workshops to determine differences in their compositions.

22. The presence of uranium might cast doubt on the authenticity of the piece; however, it should be noted here that uranium ores do occur in this region of France and thus its early exploitation as a colorant should not be ruled out before more scientific analyses of similar pieces become available for comparison. Uranium is present also in the green and yellow of a nineteenth-century *cloisonné* enamel on gold (no. A1) and in the green of a clasp (no. A6).

23. *"Mappae Clavicula* – A Key to the World of Medieval Techniques,"* translated by C.S. Smith and J. G. Hawthorne, *Transactions of the American Philosophical Society* 64, part 4 (1974).

24. Where tin-oxide-opacified white enamel is encountered, either on its own or added to modify a stronger

color, tin is present in readily detectable amounts. Tin sometimes occurs as well in enamels colored by copper. In these cases it is believed that it derives from the use of bronze or of bronze corrosion products; the ratio of copper to tin contents would be expected to reflect this source (E. V. Sayre, personal communication).

25. It must be stressed that tin is observed in the white enamel of Limoges pieces and in those colors modified with white. Antimony is sometimes apparent also in the blue, green, or red areas of the same piece, possibly because the colors might have been mixed with tin-oxide white before firing. The presence of such mixtures can be clarified by microscopic examination. These observations imply a continued, if limited, use of Roman materials. Limoges enamelers added tin-oxide-opacified white to stretch and extend a dwindling resource.

26. For instance, the analyses of the colorants and opacifiers of an English casket (no. 3) follow the pattern of the Limoges (or Cologne) School in that calcium-antimonate-opacified enamels are present alongside those opacified with tin oxide. This mixing of old with new materials by the enamelers might be clarified with more analyses, specifically of the alkaline component of the glass matrix; glass and enamel made in northern Europe would be expected to have a high potassium content relative to reused Roman material or to that imported from Byzantium.

Fig. 1. Detail of a colonnette showing the thin reaction layer of red copper oxide at the metal-enamel interface, typically found on *champlevé* enamels (see no. 16).

Fig. 2. Detail illustrating *basse-taille* enameling (see no. 40).

Fig. 3. (a) A stereobinocular microscope reveals the chisel marks made at the edges of the enamel field. (See no. 16, one of four colonnettes.)

Fig. 3. (b) Where enamel has been lost from the base of the field, tool marks are readily visible with low magnification (see no. 3).

Fig. 6. A microphoto shows an example of a mixed-color *champlevé* field (see no. 12). The medieval craftsman used the hollow quill of a goose feather to empty the enamel into the recesses. Theophilus makes no mention of the use of any binding material at this stage but some adhesive for the powdered enamel, such as gum or honey, must have been required for the preparation of objects of any curvature.

Fig. 7. (a) The reserved areas of copper were frequently decorated with engraved designs (see no. 27).

Fig. 7. (b) Inscriptions and details of figures might be highlighted by blue enamel within the surface engraving (see no. 15).

Fig. 11. The microphoto illustrates the semitranslucent purple enamel and other colors on an English casket (see no. 3).

Fig. 9. An example of blue with white powdered enamel mixed prior to fusion (see no. 5)

Fig. 12. The microphoto shows the lead-tin-oxide yellow of the Emly Shrine (see no. 1).

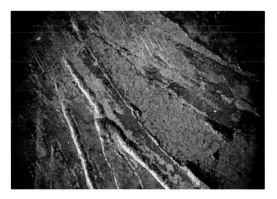

Fig. 10. The microphoto shows incompletely fused red enamel surrounded by a colorless lead glass on an enameled container of the Limoges school (see no. 33).

Fig. 13. The microphoto shows yellow enamel colored by uranium (see no. 2).

· COLOR PLATES ·

1. *Reliquary (Emly Shrine)*
   Ireland, late 7th - early 8th century

3. Casket with Beasts in Scrolls
England, third quarter of 12th century

2. Plaque with a Saint
Southwestern France, Conques (?), late 11th - early 12th century (?)

2

5. *Plaque with Three Worthies in the Fiery Furnace*
  Meuse, Maastricht (?), third quarter of 12th century

3

6. Plaque with Busts of Apostles Andrew and Philip
Meuse, third quarter of 12th century

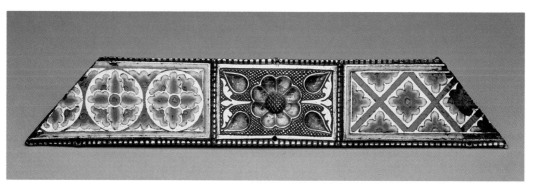

8. Ornamental Plaque
Rhineland or Meuse, last third of 12th century

7. *Hanging Reliquary*
   Meuse, third quarter of 12th century

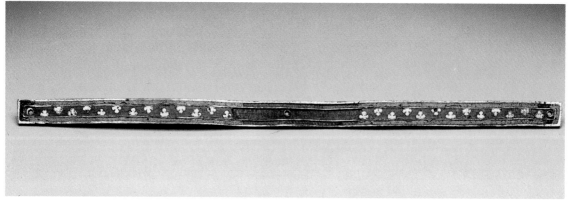

10. *Ornamental Plaque*
Rhineland or Meuse or North Germany, last third of 12th century

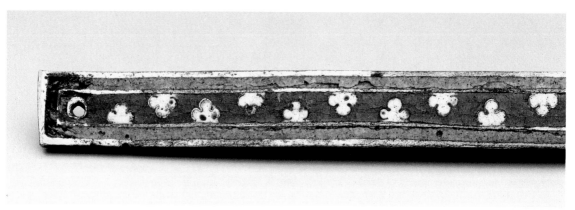

10. Detail

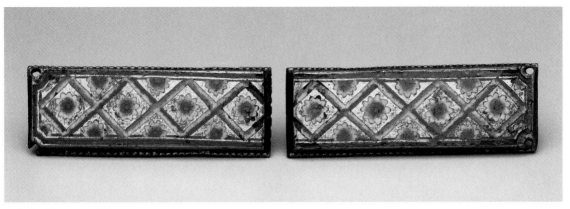

12. *Pair of Ornamental Plaques*
   Rhineland or Meuse, last quarter of 12th century

11. *Ornamental Lunette*
   Rhineland or Meuse, ca. 1170

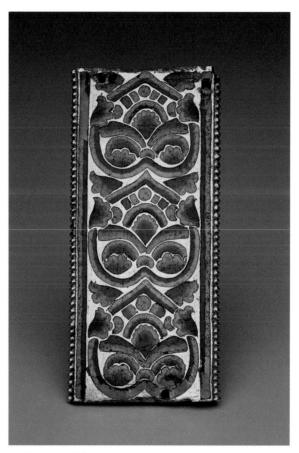

9. *Ornamental Plaque*
   Cologne, ca. 1160-1170

14. *Halo*
   Cologne, ca. 1183

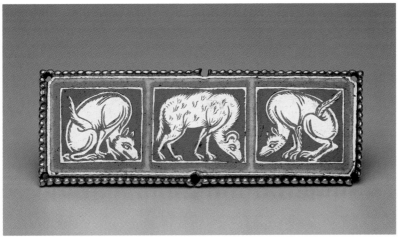

15. *Plaque with Beasts*
   Cologne, ca. 1185

9

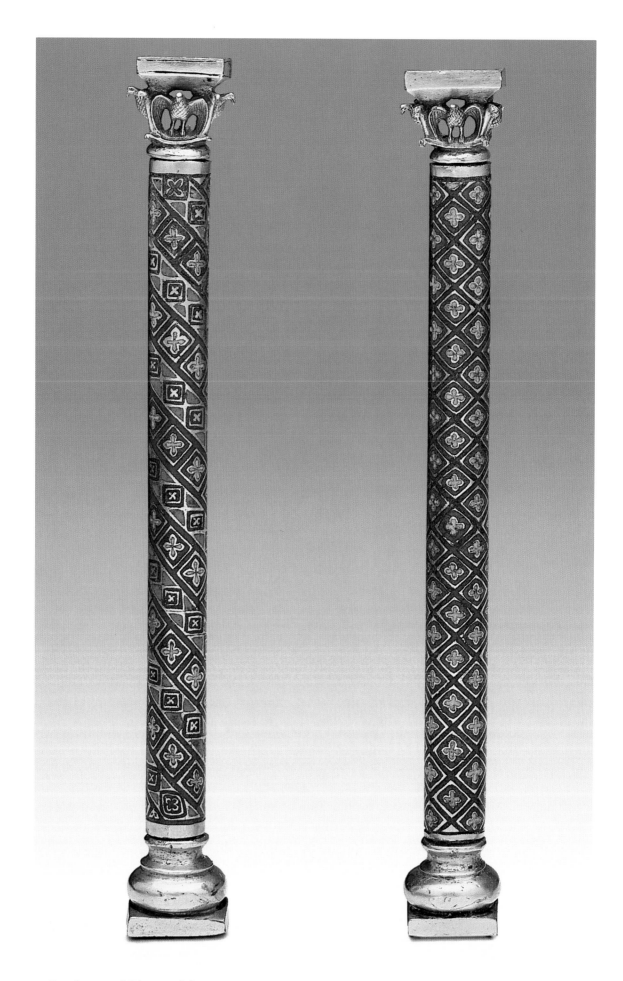

16. *Four Ornamental Colonnettes*. Cologne, ca. 1185

17. *Ornamental Plaque*
   Cologne, ca. 1186

20. *Plaque with Busts of Four Angels*
   Cologne, ca. 1220-1230

19. *Ornamental Plaque*
   Cologne, late 12th-early 13th century

21. *Plaque with Two Apostles in Medallions*
   North Germany, last quarter of 12th century

23. *Relief of Christ*
Limoges, ca. 1210

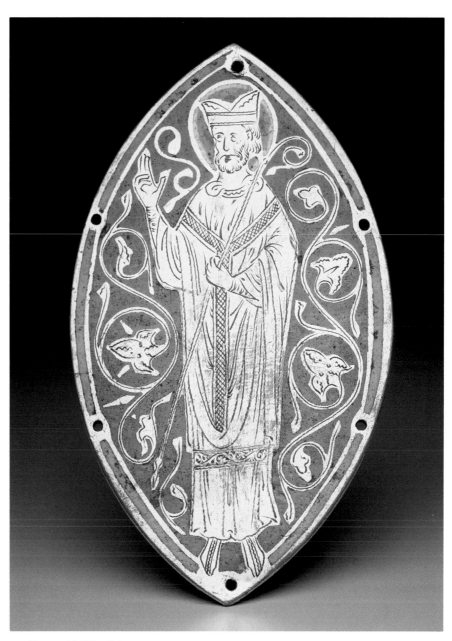

24. *Plaque with Bishop Saint*
   Limoges, first quarter of 13th century

26. *Eucharistic Dove*
   Limoges, first half of 13th century

29. *Pyx*
Limoges, first half of 13th century

28. *Pyx*
Limoges, first half of 13th century

30. *Roundel with Basilisks*
Limoges, first half of 13th century

27. *Box with Busts of Angels*
Limoges, first half of 13th century (with modern lid)

32. *Relief of Baptism of Christ*
   Limoges, mid-13th century

33. *Circular Hinged Case*
    Limoges or Limoges workshop in Paris, third quarter of 13th century

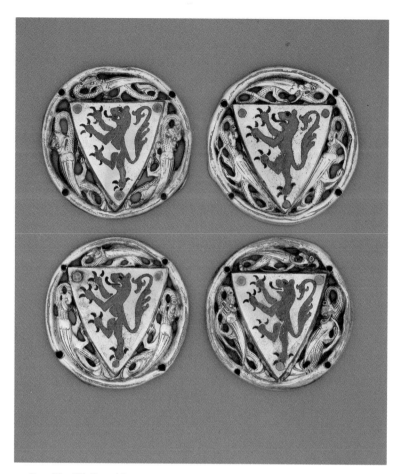

34. *Four Heraldic Roundels*
    Limoges, third quarter of 13th century

36. *Pair of Plaques with Beasts*
   Limoges or Limoges workshop in England, ca. 1300

38. *Reliquary Triptych with the Crucifixion, Coronation of
the Virgin, Saint Peter and Saint Paul, and the Annunciation*
Paris or England, early 14th century

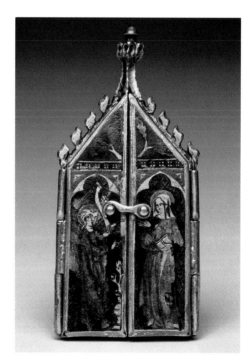

38. (wings closed)

39. *Container with Saint John the Baptist and*
    Noli me Tangere
    Paris (?), second or third quarter of 14th century (?)

39.

41. *Quatrefoil Plaque of Christ's Descent into Limbo*
    Upper Rhineland (?), late 14th century (?)

40. *Oval Plaque with Saint Edmund and Angels*
   England (?), late 14th century (?)

42. *Escutcheon of the Arte della Lana*
   Florence, late 14th century

43. *Spoon with Fox in Ecclesiastical Garb Preaching to Geese*
   South Netherlands, ca. 1430

44. *Quatrefoil Plaque with Angel Holding Instruments of the Passion*
France, mid-15th century

45. *Triptych Pendant with Martyrdom of Saint Barbara, Mary Magdalene,*
and Saint Gereon
Cologne, 1504

46. *Buckle Plate*
   Northern France, Belgium or Rhineland, ca. 480-520

47. *Circular Brooch*
   Italy, first half of 7th century

52. *Seven Glass Plaques*
Italy, Venice (?), late 13th century (?)

· CATALOGUE ·

The catalogue is comprehensive, with the exception of a group of small fragments of stained glass. These will be published in the forthcoming volume of the *Corpus vitrearum medii aevi* on American collections. Descriptions of the enamels include a sentence listing the steps involved in the production of the piece and one giving the enamel colors. These are intended to facilitate comparison with related objects in the *Catalogue international de l'oeuvre de Limoges*, where this information will be provided in a similar manner.

Problematic pieces have been included in the main body of the catalogue and are indicated by a question mark after the date and place of origin. Objects of doubtful authenticity are appended at the end.

For the place of origin, often a city or specific region is given; at other times, only a country can be provided. Dates are as precise as possible. In a few instances our piece is a fragment from a datable object; otherwise more general dates (especially for the Limoges objects that await comprehensive study) have been assigned on the basis of related pieces. Only one object (no. 45) is dated by an inscription.

Measurements, given in millimeters and inches, are listed as follows: H indicates the greatest height; W designates the greatest width. For three-dimensional objects D is the greatest depth; for circular objects DIAM indicates the diameter. Under provenance, both private collectors (with dates of their public sales) and dealers are included.

All bibliography is abbreviated; the list of abbreviations appears on page 159. Abbreviated citations among the exhibitions refer to a catalogue; when exhibitions are not abbreviated, a catalogue was not produced.

RELIQUARY (EMLY SHRINE)
Ireland, late 7th – early 8th century
Champlevé enamel on bronze over yew wood;
gilt-bronze moldings, inlay of lead-tin alloy
H: 92 mm. (3¹¹⁄₁₆ in.) L: 105 mm. (4³⁄₁₆ in.)
W: 41 mm. (1¹¹⁄₁₆ in.)
52.1396   *Theodora Wilbour Fund in Memory of
Charlotte Beebe Wilbour*

PROVENANCE: William Monsell of Tervoe (Lord
Emly), Limerick, Ireland

BIBLIOGRAPHY: Westwood 1868, p. 151; Murphy
1892, p. 151; Petersen 1907, p. 15; Armstrong 1922,
pp. 135-136; Crawford 1923, pp. 84-85; Braun 1940,
p. 199; Mahr 1941, pp. 107-110, pl. 17:1; G.
Swarzenski 1954, pp. 50-63; Henry 1956, p. 84; *Boston Museum Bulletin* 1957, p. 61, no. 6; Marstrander
1963, p. 6; H. Swarzenski 1969, pp. 484-486, no. 1;
Mancinelli 1973, pp. 253-254; Horat 1982, p. 63, fig.
10

EXHIBITIONS: "Exhibition of 1853," Royal Irish
Academy, Dublin, 1853; New York 1977, p. 137, no.
31

DESCRIPTION: Carved from a single block of wood,
the body and lid have bronze moldings (applied with
small nails) on the edges. Attached to the ridgepole of
the sloped roof are bird's-head terminals in green,
yellow, and red (now brown) enamel and a central
boss – repeating the shape of the shrine – with a grid
of yellow and green enamel. Only the front is decorated with thin strips of a lead-tin alloy hammered into
a repetitive step pattern around central crosses
engraved in the wood and with three medallions with
yellow and green enamel arranged in a geometric pattern of concentric circles. There are two hinges on the
back and an interior clasp on the front.

CONDITION: Two holes on both narrow sides indicate that hinges for mounting a leather strap are missing. The back side of the body has been replaced with
new wood and the hinges are modern. Central settings
of the medallions, as revealed by traces of mounting
paste, are lacking. Areas of the inlaid design are missing, and the wood is damaged in places, especially in
the front left corner. The red enamel has turned brown
as a result of devitrification.

The Emly Shrine belongs to a group of nine
reliquaries of similar size, shape, and construction.[1] A number of fragments,[2] primarily ridgepoles and medallions, indicate that there were
many more reliquaries of this type. They are
thought to have been hung around the neck or

shoulder.[3] Their decoration is clearly Insular, and the provenance of several of them accounts for their assignment to Ireland. Both the Loch Erne and Shannon shrines were discovered in the Irish rivers whose names they bear, and the Copenhagen and Melhus shrines, although found in Viking graves in Scandinavia, were probably looted from Irish monasteries.[4]

The reliquary most closely approximating the Emly Shrine is the one in the monastery of San Salvatore in central Italy. While engraved metal plates cover the surface of the others, only these two have inlaid geometric patterns on the front. The inlaid stepped pattern on the Emly Shrine is a common Insular motif found in contemporary Northumbrian and Irish manuscripts like the Lindisfarne Gospels, the Durham Cassiodorus, and the Book of Kells.[5] Another feature shared by the Emly and San Salvatore shrines (like one from Bologna and a dismembered ridgepole from Roscommon[6]) are zoomorphic terminals on the ridgepoles. The large circular terminals on those of the other shrines are a simplification of zoomorphic forms and may be seen as a later development. Thus, the Emly, San Salvatore, and Bologna shrines are probably the earliest of the Irish house-shaped reliquaries, all of which are datable on stylistic grounds between the end of

the seventh century and the beginning of the ninth.[7]

1. For descriptions of the Loch Erne, Melhus, Copenhagen, Shannon, and Monymusk shrines see Mahr 1941, pp. 106-110; 113-114; for the San Salvatore Shrine see Mancinelli 1973, pp. 251-256; for the Setnes shrine see Marstrander 1963, pp. 1-36; and for the Bologna shrine see the forthcoming publication of Martin Blindheim, "The House-Shaped Irish-Scots Reliquary in the Museo Civico Medievale in Bologna and its Place among the Other Reliquaries," *Acta Archaeologia* 55 (1985).

2. See Mahr 1941, pp. 110-113. Recently, Michael Ryan has discovered a roof plate in the Musée Cinquantenaire in Brussels (publication forthcoming). The authors are grateful for his assistance with this entry.

3. See G. Swarzenski 1954, p. 54.

4. Ibid., p. 52. Indeed a runic inscription incised on the bottom of the Copenhagen Shrine has been shown to have epigraphic features in common with those on monumental crosses on the Isle of Man.

5. The manuscripts are in the British Library, London (Cotton Nero D. IV, folio 2v); the Cathedral Library, Durham (B. II. 30, folio 172v); and Trinity College, Dublin (MS A. 1.6 [58], folio 4v). See Alexander 1978, pp. 35-40, 46, 71-76, nos. 9, 17, 52.

6. See Mahr 1941, p. 111.

7. See Marstrander 1963, pp. 10-14.

PLAQUE WITH A SAINT
Southwestern France, Conques (?), late 11th – early 12th century (?)
Cloisonné enamel and gilding on copper
H: 64 mm. (2½ in.) W: 46 mm. (1¹³⁄₁₆ in.)
49.471 *William Francis Warden Fund*

PROVENANCE: Paul Garnier, Paris; Joseph Brummer, New York (sale, Parke-Bernet, April 23, 1949, no. 699, ill. p. 183)

BIBLIOGRAPHY: *Boston Museum Bulletin* 1957, p. 78, no. 29; Gauthier 1966, p. 83; Gauthier 1985, no. 28

EXHIBITIONS: Arras 1935, no. 155, p. 27, pl. 20; Boston 1940, no. 231, p. 68; Cleveland 1967, no. II 9, pp. 38-39

DESCRIPTION: Half-length *cloisonné* figure in a shallow copper box made of two pieces. It is gilded on the front and sides, and the *cloisons* are attached to a base plate whose edges, bent to form the sides, are soldered to an upper plate that has been cut to frame the enamel. A shallow impression of the enamel appears on the reverse of the base plate. Radiographs (fig. 14) show that the enamel extends under the frame cut in the top plate. Enamel colors are lapis blue, turquoise, red, yellow, and a flesh tone (a mixture of red and white). The frontal saint with a yellow halo is shown half-length, wearing a lapis-blue tunic with red cuffs and yellow and red bands at the neck. He holds a closed red book in his left hand. Surrounding his right hand is a turquoise area with curved *cloisons*. Single *cloisons* define both the long wavy hair and the contour of the face. A lock of hair, formed by a looped *cloison*, projects onto the forehead. One *cloison* also forms the eyebrows and nose and each of the eyes, which are lapis blue. An upper and a lower *cloison* outline the mouth.

CONDITION: Much of the gilding has been abraded on the copper *cloisons* and in areas on the front and sides. There are small losses of enamel on the edges and several areas of what may be enamel repairs: on the book, the neckband, the right cheek and at the bottom of the turquoise area around the right hand. The small attachment hole on the upper edge is probably not original.

The simplicity of the *cloisonné* design and the limited palette are peculiar to a small group of enamels imitating Byzantine models, made in southwestern France about 1100.¹ Central to the group are those depicting Christ, the Evangelist symbols, and various saints on the portable altar

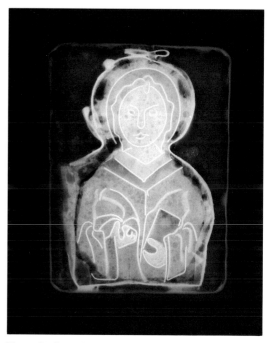

Fig. 14. Radiograph.

of Saint Foy in the treasury of Conques Abbey.² Probably one of the numerous examples of precious metalwork donated by its abbot Begon III (1087-1107), the altar may well have been made in a monastic workshop at Conques. Executed in a similar manner, and thus possibly from the same workshop as the Conques altar, are a pair of roundels in Rouen³ and Antwerp⁴ (one with a bust of Hosea and the other with a bust of Moses), a mandorla-shaped plaque with a standing female martyr in Paris,⁵ a roundel showing a seated elder in New York,⁶ and a roundel with a bust of the Virgin in Baltimore.⁷ Like the enamels on the Conques altar, the Boston saint was probably mounted on a more complex structure, either a portable altar or a book cover.

The other members of this group, like the present enamel, are composed of a base plate to which *cloisons* are attached and a top plate from which the design is cut out. Unrecorded for the other pieces but present on the Boston and Baltimore⁸ enamels is a bottom plate curved to form a box, thereby creating between the two plates an empty space where there is no enamel. If examination of the other enamels reveals this to be a feature unique to the Boston and Baltimore pieces, then their authenticity would be in question. Additional reasons for doubting the authenticity of the Boston enamel are the presence of uranium in the yellow enamel[9] and the saint's tunic with the curious turquoise inset, which might be explained as a forger's misunderstanding of the customary tunic and pallium.

1. See Gauthier 1966, pp. 82-84; Gauthier 1972, pp. 72-78.

2. See Gauthier 1972, p. 326, fig. 34; Avril et al. 1983, pp. 317-318, fig. 280.

3. Musée des antiquités de la Seine Maritime acc. no. 723C. See Gauthier 1972, p. 326; fig. 35.

4. Musée Meyer Van den Bergh acc. no. 455 (419). See Gauthier 1972, p. 326, fig. 36.

5. Musée du Louvre acc. no. OA 6273. See Avril et al. 1983, p. 317, fig. 281.

6. Metropolitan Museum of Art acc. no. 1983.38. See New York 1983, p. 17.

7. Walters Art Gallery acc. no. 44.152. See Ross 1939, p. 476.

8. The authors are grateful to Gary Vikan and the members of the Research Laboratory at the Walters Art Gallery for examining this piece in detail.

9. With one possible exception in a Roman mosaic, that element has not been reported as a colorant in glasses before the nineteenth century (see p. xxii). According to Marie-Madeleine Gauthier (oral communication), however, uranium is abundant in the soil in Conques and the surrounding area, and may prove to exist in other medieval enamels from this region.

CASKET WITH BEASTS IN SCROLLS
England, third quarter of 12th century
Champlevé enamel and gilding on copper
H: 61 mm. (2⅜ in.) W: 109 mm. (4⁵⁄₁₆ in.)
D: 68 mm. (2¹¹⁄₁₆ in.)
52.1381   *Helen and Alice Colburn Fund*

PROVENANCE: DeBruge-Dumenil, Paris (sale, Paris, 1850); Peter Soltykoff, Paris (sale, Hôtel Drouot, April 8, 1861, no. 91); Mannheim (sale, April 17, 1868, no. 1); Jules Frésart, Liège; Otto Wertheimer, Paris

BIBLIOGRAPHY: Labarte 1847, p. 581, no. 680; *Boston Museum Bulletin* 1957, p. 78, no. 28; Gauthier 1964, p. 152 n. 37; Campbell 1979, p. 367, fig. 48; Gauthier 1979, p. 82, fig. 4

EXHIBITIONS: Liège 1905, no. 279, pl. 14; Liège 1930, no. 179; New York 1970, no. 170, pp. 164, 176; London 1984, no. 284, p. 269; Stratford 1984, p. 213 n. 26

DESCRIPTION: Rectangular box constructed from four side plaques, a base plate, and a beveled lid. Hammered, *champlevé*, engraved, punched, enameled, soldered, and gilded. The underside of the lid and the bottom of the base are gilded; enamel colors are yellow, yellow green, apple green, lapis blue, light gray blue, white, turquoise (two shades), red, and translucent purple in fields of up to five colors. On the central plaque of the lid, against a punched gold ground, intertwined tendrils, symmetrically arranged around a central hole, sprout multicolored, scalloped blossoms of various shapes. On the sloping sides of the lid against a blue ground, bifurcated tendrils, gilded and punched, form medallions (four on the long sides and two on the short sides) around their blossoms. Translucent purple and apple green alternate as grounds for the varied multicolored blossoms. Their curled edges, chased and in reserve, pass alternately above and under the medallions. Intersecting tendrils are marked by knots.

The sides of the box show, on a lapis-blue ground, a continuous acanthus scroll, again punched and in reserve, with simple, curled leaves, some of which are enameled. Emerging from a single stem, the branches develop into medallions and divide either to form a branch for the next medallion or to sprout narrower tendrils with curved leaves to fill the interstices. In the medallions (three on the front and back and two on the sides), a turquoise ground surrounds various beasts in reserve: on the front are a quadruped with a monkey's head and cap, two facing goats on their hind legs, a quadruped with donkey ears; on the right side are two affronted griffins; on the back are a lion, rabbit, and centaur with a bow; and on the left side are two addorsed quadrupeds.

CONDITION: The four turned feet are modern. Missing are the two hinges and the front clasp, for which there are several holes, some of them now plugged. The hole in the center of the lid was probably for a handle. A crack in the right front corner of the roof has been repaired with a staple. There are large losses from the lapis-blue and turquoise enamel grounds, and the gilding is considerably abraded.

Probably made for secular use, this small box belongs to a group of enameled objects that includes three ciboria (referred to by the names of their former owners: Morgan, Balfour, and Warwick),[1] two crosier heads (the Chartres and Whithorn crosiers),[2] four small caskets (the Troyes, Fitzwilliam, Liberal Arts, and Bargello caskets),[3] and a badly mutilated fragment from the side of another casket.[4] Although the objects differ somewhat in style, and, in fact, have been dated variously between about 1150 and 1200, they appear close enough in technique and design to suggest origin in a common workshop tradition. The number of workshops and hands involved in their production, however, is still to be determined.

The palette of colored enamels on the Boston box is comparable to that of the others in the group with the exception of its translucent purple and light blue gray, which are unique. The beasts, a common feature of contemporary English manuscripts and sculptural decoration,[5] are a curious mixture of signs of the zodiac (most likely derived from calendar illustrations) and other animals, both fantastic and real, probably based on contemporary bestiary illustrations.[6] (Both the Chartres and Whithorn crosiers show a similar variety of exotic beasts.) The *rinceaux* on the sides of the box are closely related to those on the knop of the Chartres crosier and the bowls of the three ciboria. The large and varied blossoms framing the lid also resemble those on the ciboria, especially on the bowl of the ciborium in the Morgan Library, where the stems encircle the blossoms in a similar manner. Likewise, the interlaced branches and blossoms in the center of

37

the lid are akin to those on the bases and knobs of the ciboria. The very closest comparisons for both the sides (see radiograph, fig. 4) and the lid design, however, are found in manuscripts: for the former, the Majesty page of the Bury Bible (a manuscript thought to have been written at Bury Saint Edmunds about 1135 [7]), and for the latter, the decorative initials in the Eadwine Psalter, written at Canterbury about 1150-1160.[8]

It is likely that the box was produced in the same workshop as the ciboria, whose inscriptions and iconography suggest origin in the West Country. Its close relationship to both the ciboria and the manuscripts supports a date no later than the third quarter of the century.

1. Morgan ciborium: Pierpont Morgan Library, New York; Balfour ciborium: Victoria and Albert Museum, London, acc. no. M.1.1981; Warwick ciborium: Victoria and Albert Museum acc. no. M.159-1919. (See London 1984, pp. 263-265, nos. 278-280; Stratford 1984, pp. 204-216.) This whole group has been assigned to England, in part on the basis of the typological inscriptions on the ciboria, which are identical to those forming part of the twelfth-century decoration of the Chapter House at Worcester Cathedral.

2. Chartres crosier: Museo nazionale del Bargello, Florence, acc. no. 662C; Whithorn crosier: National Museum of Antiquities of Scotland, Edinburgh, acc. no. KC 1982. See London 1984, pp. 266-267, 269-270, nos. 282, 285; Campbell 1979, pp. 364-369; Oman 1967, pp. 299-300.

3. Troyes casket: Troyes Cathedral Treasury; Fitzwilliam casket: Fitzwilliam Museum, Cambridge, acc. no. M.27.1904; Liberal Arts casket: Victoria and Albert Museum, London, acc. no. M.7955. 1862; Bargello casket: Museo nazionale del Bargello, Florence, acc. no. 652C. See London 1984, pp. 267-268, 270-271, nos. 283, 287, 288; H. Swarzenski 1954, fig. 489.

4. Winchester City Museum acc. no. BS.SF.153. See London 1984, p. 270, no. 286.

5. Compare especially the doorway at Saint Mary's, Barfeston (Kent). See Zarnecki 1953, p. 60, pls. 87-90.

6. See London 1984, p. 269.

7. Corpus Christi College, Cambridge, MS 2, f. 281v. See Kauffmann 1975, pp. 88-90, no. 56.

8. Trinity College Library, Cambridge, MS R.17.1, folio 91r. See Kauffmann 1975, pp. 96-97, no. 68.

4

RELIQUARY WITH ENTHRONED CHRIST
(OBVERSE) AND
VIRGIN AND CHILD (REVERSE)
England or Lower Saxony, mid-12th century
Champlevé enamel and gilding on copper
H: 60 mm. (2⁷/₁₆ in.) W: 60 mm. (2⁷/₁₆ in.)
D: 6 mm. (⁵/₁₆ in.)
55.466 *Harriet Otis Cruft Fund*

PROVENANCE: Crodel, Halle; Phillip Nelson, Liverpool; Herbert Bier, London

DESCRIPTION: Quadrilobed container with an opening and two holes at the top, probably for an attachment loop. The front, showing an enthroned Christ, was hammered, engraved, and gilded. The very damaged back plaque, depicting a Madonna and Child, was hammered, *champlevé*, engraved, enameled, and gilded. A single strip of copper soldered to the plaques forms the sides.

With an open book in his left hand and his right hand raised in benediction, the long-haired and bearded Christ sits on a backless throne with a crosshatched cushion. The ground is diapered with the central circle marked in reserve. On the back, within a central circle, the half-length Virgin in reserve holds the Child in her left arm and a flowering rod in her right hand. To judge from the remaining traces of enamel, the Virgin's halo and the ground within the circle were lapis blue. Christ's halo and the lobes of the quatrefoil were white.

CONDITION: The original gilding is almost completely abraded and that remaining on the front may be modern. The back, with only minute traces of enamel in very shallow fields, is rubbed.

Small reliquaries of this type, whose shape probably derives from larger reliquaries like that of Henry II in the Louvre[1] (made in Lower Saxony, ca. 1170), were probably hung around the neck. The present example is nearly identical in size and technique to two others whose figure style is clearly Lower Saxon: one in the Vatican[2] having the same iconography and another in Halberstadt[3] showing Christ surrounded by the symbols of the Evangelists on one side and the Crucifixion on the other. If in type then, the Boston reliquary seems to be Lower Saxon, it is more closely allied in its figure style to English examples of the mid-twelfth century, especially the Christ in Majesty in the Bury Bible (ca. 1135).[4] This English damp-fold drapery style was imported to Lower Saxony after the marriage in 1168 of Henry the Lion to Mathilde (daughter of Henry II of England),[5] and thus allows for the possibility that the present reliquary could be Lower Saxon.

1. Acc. no. D 70-72. See Gauthier 1972, p. 359, no. 108; Stuttgart 1977, pp. 445-446, no. 575.
2. Museo Sacro acc. no. 849. See Stohlman 1939, p. 28, no. 85.
3. Cathedral Treasury; unpublished.
4. Corpus Christi College, Cambridge, MS 2, f. 281v. See Kauffmann 1975, pp. 88-90, no. 56.
5. An example is the Oswald reliquary in Hildesheim. See Lasko 1972, p. 207.

PLAQUE WITH THREE WORTHIES IN THE
FIERY FURNACE

Meuse, Maastricht (?), third quarter of 12th
century

Champlevé enamel and gilding on copper

H: 208 mm. (8³⁄₁₆ in.) DIAM.: 227 mm. (8¹⁵⁄₁₆
in.)

51.7 *William Francis Warden Fund*

PROVENANCE: Countess Dzialynska, Paris; Prince
Wladyslaw Czartoryski, Goluchow Castle, Poznan,
Poland; J. Pollack, Paris; Wildenstein and Company,
New York

BIBLIOGRAPHY: de Laborde 1853, p. 41 n. 1; Darcel
1865, pp. 514-515; Burty 1869, p. 228; Giraud 1881,
pl. 4; de Linas 1881, pp. 189-190; Molinier 1900, pp.
148, 151; Molinier 1903, p. 33, fig. 127, pl. 2; Von
Falke and Frauberger 1904, p. 73 n. 3; H. Swarzenski
1953, p. 157; H. Swarzenski 1954, pp. 29, 31, 69, fig.
368, pl. 167; *Boston Museum Bulletin* 1957, frontispiece; Paris 1957, no. 109, pp. 68-69; H. Swarzenski
1958, pp. 30-49, fig. 1; Green 1961, pp. 157-169,
figs. 1, 2, 3, 5; H. Swarzenski 1969, p. 488; Verdier
1970, p. 15, no. 50; Gauthier 1972, pp. 136, 350, fig.
94; Brodsky 1972, pp. 23-24, fig. 11; Kötzsche
1973a, pp. 193, 204-206, pl. 15; Morgan 1973, p.
266; Verdier 1975, pp. 69-74; Buschhausen 1980, p.
95

EXHIBITIONS: "Exposition de l'Union Centrale des
Beaux-Arts appliqués à l'industrie," Paris, 1865, no.
196; "Exposition de l'Union Centrale des Beaux-Arts
appliqués à l'industrie," Paris, 1880. no. 1; Stuttgart
1977, no. 552, pp. 418-419, fig. 352

DESCRIPTION: Slightly convex plaque shaped like a
scale with beaded border on the round edge and six
pinholes. Hammered, tooled, *champlevé*, enameled, and
gilded. Enamel colors are lapis blue (two shades),
azure blue, light blue, white, turquoise, yellow, green,
and red in single and mixed fields of up to three colors.
A bending angel (inscribed ANGEL[US]) with spread
wings and arms strikes the flames from the furnace
with the three Worthies, Ananias, Azarias, and Misael.
They carry a scroll inscribed with their song:
BENEDICT[US] ES D[OMI]NE D[EU]S PATRU[M]
NOSTROR[UM] ET GLORIOS[US] I[N] S[AE]C[U]LA.
With azure-blue halos edged in turquoise, the Worthies, dressed in lapis-blue tunics, stand against a gold
ground under a lapis-blue scalloped arch and red and
turquoise flames. With a cross in his nimbus, Azarias,
frontal and in the center, wears a turquoise ephod
studded with jewels. The angel, with a turquoise halo
edged in light blue and white, has a gold crown with

flying ribbons. His tunic is modeled in yellow, green,
turquoise, and lapis blue, and his mantle, with a semi-
rosette on the thigh, has folds shaded from lapis blue
to white. In his wings, each row of feathers is differ-
ently colored, starting from the top: lapis blue, lighter
lapis blue, turquoise, green, and light blue and white.
Hair is lapis blue with curls outlined in reserve; flesh is
white, and faces are all drawn according to the same
formula. The almond-shaped eyes have lapis-blue dots;
mouths are red, bordered by two parallel lines in
reserve. Bound on the outside by a lapis-blue border
with stylized leaves outlined in reserve and on the
inside by a narrow white band, the scene is described
by an inscription: NEC PUEROS LEDIT VESANI REGIS
ET IGNIS. NEC MATRIS NATUS DISOLUIT CLAUSTRA
PUDORIS.

CONDITION: There are small losses of enamel, primarily on the border. Gilding is abraded, especially at the
top of the plaque.

This unusually large plaque depicts the Angel of
God protecting the three Hebrews in the flaming
furnace. Refusing to serve Babylonian gods or to
worship the golden image erected by Nebuchad-
nezzar, Ananias, Azarias, and Misael were,
according to Daniel 3: 21, "bound in their mantles, their tunics, and their hats, and their other
garments, and they were cast into the burning
fiery furnace." The basis for the present scene is
Daniel 3: 52: "But the angel of the lord came
down into the furnace together with Azarias and
his fellows, and he smote the flame of the fire out
of the furnace, and made the midst of the furnace
as it had been a moist whistling wind, so that the
fire touched them not at all, neither hurt nor
troubled them. Then the three, as out of one
mouth, praised and glorified, and blessed God in
the furnace, saying (as written here on the
scroll): "Blessed art thou, O Lord, thou God of
our father, and to be praised and exalted above
all forever."

The unique composition of the scene, the rich
graduated tones, and the precision and intricacy
of the *champlevé* design reveal the work of a great
master. Occupying nearly half the plaque, the
monumental angel with spread wings derives
from a Byzantine model. Individual features –
including the flying ribbons of the angel's crown,
the half-rosette on his thigh, the turning of his

foot to reveal the sole, and the oval faces – are paralleled among Mosan metalwork and manuscript painting of the third quarter of the twelfth century. Comparison with the Shrine of Saint Servatius in Maastricht (ca. 1160), specifically the monumental angels with spread wings and the figures in roundels holding bowed bands with inscriptions on the roof, suggests Maastricht as the place of origin.[1]

A second scale-shaped plaque in the Musée des Beaux-Arts in Lille,[2] narrower than the Boston plaque, but also slightly convex and with nearly the same diameter, belongs to the same ensemble. Here Gideon stands beside the Fleece of Wool, which the hand of God wets with dew (HIC ROS STILLAT I[N] VELLERE). The bowl [CONCA] of water wrung from the fleece is placed below. Although most of the enamel has been lost, the style of the figures, border design, and epigraphy is so close to the Boston plaque that both have been assigned to the same master.[3]

The shape of the plaques and the beading, only on the rounded edges, suggests that they were part of a larger ensemble surrounding a central plaque or pillar. The framing inscription on the Boston plaque – "Neither the fury of the King and the fire can harm the youths, nor can the birth of the Mother destroy the seal of her Virginity" – indicates that the scene was conceived as a type of the Incarnation. With the wet fleece on dry ground, the story of Gideon is also an Old Testament prefiguration of the same New Testament theme. Thus, the plaques probably adjoined one showing the Virgin and Child and, like the polylobed ensemble shown in the seventeenth-century drawing of the lost retable of Saint Remaclus in Stavelot,[4] were mounted on an altar retable dedicated to the Virgin.

Two reconstructions for this original ensemble have been proposed. The first and simpler design is an unequal quatrefoil composed of four scale-shaped plaques surrounding a square. Here the Boston plaque is on the bottom and the Lille plaque is placed on the right. Daniel among the lions who cannot harm him and God appearing to Moses in the Burning Bush (both of which are also Old Testament prefigurations for the Virgin Birth) may have been represented on the other sides. The same iconographic ensemble surrounds an enthroned Virgin and Child in an early-twelfth-century miniature showing the Tree of Jesse in the Cîteaux Lectionary in Dijon.[5]

A more complex quatrefoil, consisting of sixteen plaques around a central image of the Incarnation, has also been proposed.[6] There are several equally extensive typological programs of contemporary date. In this reconstruction the orientation of the plaques would be rotated forty-five degrees.

The suggestion that this larger quatrefoil formed part of the base of the great cross commissioned by Abbot Suger for Saint Denis before 1147 cannot be substantiated, as descriptions of the cross do not mention such scenes on the base.[7] It has also been proposed that a circular plaque of the Adoration of the Magi in Paris,[8] with a border pattern similar to those on the Boston and Lille plaques, may have been at the center of the ensemble. Differences in style and color and the lower quality of this roundel, however, argue against that hypothesis.

1. See H. Swarzenski 1958, pp. 36-37.

2. Acc. no. A54. See Stuttgart 1977, pp. 418-419, no. 552; Cologne 1985, vol. 1, p. 298, no. B85.

3. See H. Swarzenski 1958, p. 47.

4. The retable was commissioned by Abbot Wibald, who died in 1158. See Gauthier 1972, pp. 345-346, no. 83

5. Bibliothèque Municipale, MS 641. See H. Swarzenski 1958, pp. 47-48.

6. See Green 1961, pp. 157-169.

7. See Verdier 1970, pp. 1-31.

8. Cluny Museum acc. no. LOA 252. See Morgan 1973, p. 266.

enlarged detail

PLAQUE WITH BUSTS OF APOSTLES ANDREW AND PHILIP

Meuse, third quarter of 12th century
Champlevé enamel and gilding on copper
H: 51 mm. (2 in.) W: 72 mm. (2⅞ in.)
47.1440 *Grace M. Edwards Fund in Memory of Juliana Cheney Edwards*

PROVENANCE: Aldo Jandolo, Rome and New York; Joseph Brummer, New York

BIBLIOGRAPHY: Rogers and Goetz 1945, p. 33; H. Swarzenski 1953, p. 157; *Boston Museum Bulletin* 1957, p. 78, no. 27; Morgan 1973, p. 268; Verdier 1975, pp. 42-44

EXHIBITIONS: Boston 1940, no. 246, pl. 29

DESCRIPTION: Slightly convex rectangular plaque with six pinholes. Hammered, *champlevé*, enameled, and gilded. Enamel colors are azure blue (two shades), light blue, green (two shades), yellow, turquoise, red, and white in single and mixed fields of up to three colors. Azure-blue and white frames enclose a three-quarter bust of an Apostle holding an open scroll with white on the curling edges and blue inscriptions from the Apostles' Creed. Reserved heads and hands are engraved and filled with blue enamel (see radiograph, fig. 5). Saint Andrew (inscribed .S[AN]C[TU]S.ANDREAS.) with curly hair and long beard, holds the passage .CELI.ET.TERRE.ET.IN.IH[ESU]M. Saint Philip (inscribed .S[AN]C[TU]S.PHILIPPUS.), balding and with a short beard, carries the following passage of the Creed: XP[ISTU]M.FILIUM.EIUS.UNICUM. Both have turquoise halos edged in white and wear a tunic and pallium. Andrew's tunic is two shades of green with yellow highlights; his pallium is two shades of azure blue with white highlights. The colors of Philip's garments are identical to Andrew's but those of tunic and pallium are reversed, and his right sleeve is lined in red with white dots.

CONDITION: There are small losses of enamel, primarily in the white and in the border.

Belonging with the Boston plaque is one of identical size and shape depicting Saints James and John in the Art Institute of Chicago[1] (fig. 15). James, on the left, holds the phrase from the Creed following Philip's on the Boston plaque, D[OMI]N[U]M.N[OST]R[U]M.QUI.CONCEPTUS.EST. The Creed continues on John's scroll: DE.SP[IRITU] .S[AN]C[T]O.NATUS.EX.MARIA. VIRGINE. According to legend, each Apostle contributed, on the

Fig. 15. Plaque with Busts of Apostles James and John. *Art Institute of Chicago*

first Pentecost, a passage of the Creed describing the essential articles of Christian belief. The depiction of Apostles with the Creed is not uncommon, especially in Rhenish and Lower Saxon art of the twelfth and thirteenth centuries.[2] The earliest example in enamel, datable about 1150, is found on the top of the portable altar of Eilbertus of Cologne in the Guelph Treasure,[3] where seated Apostles holding open scrolls with the Creed are arranged around Christ in Majesty. The long sides of the Shrine of Saint Heribert in Deutz,[4] made in Cologne about 1170, also show Apostles in relief holding open books inscribed with the Creed. Several common conventions exist for the division of the Creed into twelve articles, one for each Apostle.[5] The divisions on the Boston and Chicago plaques, like those on the Heribert Shrine, are, however, unique. Another peculiarity of the Heribert Shrine is that the Creed is incomplete. Given the short passages assigned to each Apostle on the plaques from Boston and Chicago, this is likely to have been the case here as well.

The passage held by Andrew immediately follows the beginning of the Creed: *Credo in Deum Patrem omnipotentem creatorem.* Its length suggests that it was given to one figure, probably Peter, who traditionally heads the sequence of the Apostles. The placement of a single figure before those on the two existing plaques limits the possibilities for reconstruction of their origi-

nal use. Plaques with double Apostle busts, but
of more square proportion, are arranged vertically on the wings of two Mosan triptychs containing relics of the True Cross in the Petit Palais
in Paris.[6] Such a use for the present plaques is
unlikely, both because of their rectangular shape
and because such a triptych would have had a
plaque with two Apostles above the Boston
plaque. Placement on the sides of a round object
is also improbable because the circumference,
based on the curve of the plaques, would be
extremely large: 107 cm., or the equivalent of
about fourteen of the present plaques.

It has been suggested that they formed a frame
around a central image or altar stone, as on the
Eilbertus altar.[7] The convex shape of the plaques,
however, argues against this. Most likely, the
plaques were placed in sequence around the sides
(where slightly bowed plaques would be more
plausible) of a portable altar (like no. 21). Two
plaques, each with two Apostles, could have been
attached to the long sides and one plaque with
two Apostles could have been used on the short
sides. On this altar the first Apostle, Peter, would
have been placed on the same plaque as the last.
The top of such an altar may have had scenes
from the life of Christ related to those described
in the various articles of the Creed on the sides.

The very fine, pointy features and narrow faces
on the plaques, not unlike some of those found
on two Mosan plaques showing the Baptism and
Pentecost,[8] are perhaps closest to those in a sacramentary in Cologne, probably made in Liège

about 1160-1170,[9] and appear to be unique
among contemporary Mosan enamels. The head
types, however, are related to those on the two
triptychs in Paris from the third quarter of the
twelfth century. The Boston Andrew, with short
curly hair and beard, is of a type identical to that
of Bartholomew on the triptychs. The others –
Philip, James, and John – find parallels among
the same saints on the triptychs.

1. Acc. no. 43.87. (Formerly in the Germeau Collection, Paris [sale, Hôtel Drouot, May 4-7, 1868, no.
44].) See Rogers and Goetz 1945, p. 66, no. 23;
Verdier 1975, pp. 42-44.

2. For example, the Canon Tables in the Gospels of
Henry the Lion, the frescoes at Gandersheim and
Braunschweig, and a series of plaques with busts of
Apostles now in Hanover, London, and Bamberg. See
G. Swarzenski 1932, pp. 241-395; Dinkler-von Schu-
bert 1964, pp. 69-104.

3. Kunstgewerbemuseum, Berlin, acc. no. W II. See
Kötzsche 1973b, pp. 68-70, no. 12.

4. See Schnitzler 1959, pp. 32-33, no. 26; Cologne
1985, vol. 2, pp. 314-323, no. E91.

5. See Gordon 1965, pp. 634-640.

6. Dutuit Collection acc. nos. 1237-1238. See
Gauthier 1972, p. 347, no. 85.

7. See Verdier 1975, pp. 42-44.

8. Metropolitan Museum of Art, New York, acc. nos.
17.190.430, 65.105; see Buschhausen 1980, p. 120.

9. Dombibliothek Cod. 157, fols. 17v, 19r. See
Schnitzler 1959, p. 26, no. 18; Cologne 1985, vol. 1,
pp. 442-444, no. C19.

HANGING RELIQUARY
Meuse, third quarter of 12th century
Vernis brun and gilding on copper over wooden
core; cabochons and rock crystal
H: 169 mm. (6¹¹⁄₁₆ in.) W: 106 mm. (4¼ in.)
D: 37 mm. (1⅜ in.)
49.480   *William Francis Warden Fund*

PROVENANCE: Alfred Rütschi, Zurich (sale, Galerie
Fischer, Lucerne, September 5, 1931, no. 44); Joseph
Brummer, New York (sale, Parke-Bernet, May 12,
1949, no. 369)

BIBLIOGRAPHY: Braun 1940, p. 297, no. 289; *Boston Museum Bulletin* 1957, p. 76, no. 23; New York
1970, no. 181, p. 176

DESCRIPTION: Mandorla-shaped reliquary with an
attachment loop at the top. Radiographs (fig. 16)
show a wooden core in one piece to which copper
plaques, overlapping at their edges, have been attached
with small nails. On the front side, the outer border
formed by two plaques is *vernis brun* with a simple dot
design. The sides of the raised central area are covered
with gilded copper stamped with a repeated curled
leaf; the gilded copper over the flat area is stamped
with a foliate scroll. In the center is a lozenge-shaped
plaque with a large oval rock crystal and deep-blue
cabochons in the corners. Radiographs reveal under
the crystal a square foil or cloth lining the cavity in
which the relic, a small bone, is placed. A copper sheet
stamped with a continuous vine scroll covers each side.
Attached to the back is a single *vernis brun* plaque with
a gold vine scroll around the border. More elaborate
but similar to that on the stamped sides, the vine scroll
begins from a split branch at the bottom and continues
up each side to the top, where the scrolls are linked
with a simple band. In the center, the same scroll and
elongated palmettes are arranged symmetrically around
a central rosette. The attachment loop projects from a
triangular plaque nailed to the core.

CONDITION: The gilding is somewhat abraded. The
upper attachment loop is modern. Two nails are missing on the back and the only replacement nail is on the
front in the upper left edge. A small break in the
enamel on the back has been repaired.

Reliquaries of this type were either hung around
the neck or suspended above the altar. The present example is related to four of the more usual
polylobed form[1] in the Cleveland Museum,[2] the
Hermitage in Leningrad,[3] the Cluny Museum in
Paris,[4] and the Metropolitan Museum in New
York.[5] The Leningrad and Cleveland examples
have enamels mounted on the front; the less
sumptuous Cluny and Metropolitan reliquaries,
like Boston's, have only ornamental decoration
and rock crystals on their front sides.

The unusual raised settings for the blue
cabochons on the Boston reliquary are matched
on the Cluny example. All have stampwork on
the sides and single *vernis brun* plaques on the
reverse. Although more exuberant and precise,
the latter on the Cleveland reliquary, having
many of the same foliate motifs and a similar
design with *rinceaux* surrounding a centralized
foliate design, are closest to Boston's. The two
pieces are roughly contemporary and probably
come from the same workshop. The figural
enamels on the Cleveland example suggest a date
for both in the third quarter of the twelfth century. Support for this dating is provided by the
correspondence of the *vernis brun* vine scroll on
the Boston reliquary with those on similar plaques on the Shrine of Saint Mangold in Huy
(thought to be the work of Godefroy de Huy,
about 1173)[6] and the Mosan book cover from
about 1150 on an eleventh-century sacramentary
from Mainz now in the J. Paul Getty Museum in
Malibu.[7]

1. Variants of the mandorla shape are found on reliquaries in the church of Saint Nicholas in Arras (see
Paris 1965, p. 18, no. 39) and the Musée des Beaux-Arts in Lille (acc. no. A79; see Liège 1951, no. 122).

2. Acc. no. 26.428. See Milliken 1927, pp. 51-54;
Verdier 1975, pp. 66-69.

3. Acc. no. O 171. See Lafontaine-Dosogne 1975, pp.
91-94, no. 2; Lapkovskaya 1971, p. 14, nos. 8-9.

4. Acc. no. CL 13076.

5. Anonymous loan no. L1984.55. (Formerly Thomas
Flannery, Chicago [sale, Sotheby Parke Bernet,
London, December 1, 1983, no. 10]; Alfred Rütschi,
Zurich [sale, Galerie Fischer, Lucerne, September 5,
1931, no. 45].)

6. See Von Falke and Frauberger 1904, pp. 63-64, fig.
18.

7. MS Ludwig V2, formerly in the Monastery of Saint
Alban in Namur. See von Euw and Plotzek 1979, vol.
1, pp. 223-230.

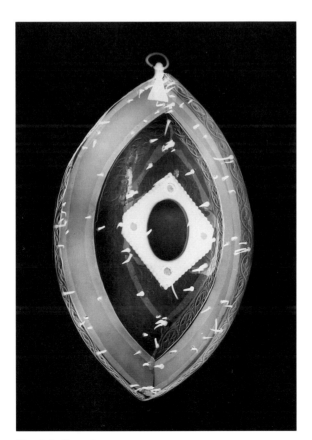

Fig. 16. Radiograph

8

ORNAMENTAL PLAQUE
Rhineland or Meuse, last third of 12th century
Champlevé enamel and gilding on copper
H: 28 mm. (1⅛ in.) W: 170 mm. (6¹¹⁄₁₆ in.)
47.1441   *Grace M. Edwards Fund in Memory of Juliana Cheney Edwards*

PROVENANCE: Paul Garnier, Paris; Joseph Brummer, New York

EXHIBITIONS: Arras 1935, p. 27, no. 154, pl. 20

DESCRIPTION: Quadrilateral plaque with two beaded edges and five tiny pinholes. Hammered, tooled, *champlevé*, enameled, engraved, chased, and gilded. Enamel colors are lapis blue, light blue, turquoise, white, green, yellow, and red in a mixed field of up to five colors. The central gilded panel is engraved with a rosette flanked by four tear-shaped cavities and two split palmettes. On the right, within a light-blue and white border, turquoise lozenges enclose full and demi-rosettes in a mixed field of (from the center out) red, turquoise, lapis blue, light blue, and white. A similar light-blue and white border on the left surrounds reserved discs containing eight-petaled rosettes with turquoise and red central circles. Green and yellow petals with red centers alternate with lapis-blue, light-blue, and white ones. Facing trefoil leaves in a mixed field of red, lapis blue, turquoise, light blue, and white fill the interstices between discs.

CONDITION: The corners have been cut, and the diagonal edges show traces of lead solder from their secondary use. There are losses of enamel on the right edge, and all the red enamel has deteriorated. The plaque has probably been regilded. Pinholes may be modern.

There are three plaques of identical size and shape (see fig. 17) in the Virginia Museum of Fine Arts in Richmond.[1] Although arranged with enamel in the center and gilded rosettes on the ends (the reverse of the Boston piece), the plaques are so close in design and execution that there can be little doubt that all four come from the same source, probably a reliquary. By 1935, when exhibited in Arras, the four were together in the collection of Paul Garnier, arranged as a frame around no. 2.[2] They are said to have formed supports originally for a cross in the Museum of Saint Omer,[3] but this statement seems to be without basis.

The four were probably cut from two longer rectangular plaques, one with beaded edges on one long side, as on the Richmond plaques, and another beaded on both long sides, as on the Boston plaque. A similar group of long enameled plaques with gilded rosettes are now divided between The Art Museum at Princeton University[4] and the Kunstgewerbemuseum in Berlin.[5]

The enamel designs on the Boston and Richmond plaques are reminiscent of those on the Shrine of Saint Albinus in Saint Pantaleon,[6] produced in Cologne about 1186 and those on the arm reliquary of Charlemagne,[7] made in Liège about 1166-1170. These comparisons suggest localization in the region of the Rhine and Meuse rivers in the last third of the twelfth century.

1. Acc. nos. 64.37.1-3. See Virginia 1966, p. 132, nos. 256-258. The authors are grateful to Dietrich Kötzsche for bringing these to their attention.

2. See Arras 1935, no. 154, pl. 20.

3. See sale catalogue, Joseph Brummer, New York (Parke-Bernet, May 14, 1949, no. 722).

4. Acc. nos. 49.121-123. (Formerly Joseph Brummer, New York [sale, Parke-Bernet, May 14, 1949, no. 726].)

5. Acc. nos. 1979.116a-d; 1984.25. (Formerly Ernest Brummer, New York [sale, Galerie Koller, Zürich, October 17, 1979, nos. 207, 213a-c, 218, 219].)

6. See Von Falke and Frauberger 1904, pl. XXII. On the shrine, see Schnitzler 1959, pp. 35-36, no. 28, pls. 101-103; Cologne 1985, vol. 2, pp. 301-303, no. E80.

7. Musée du Louvre acc. no. D712. See Stuttgart 1977, no. 538, with bibliography.

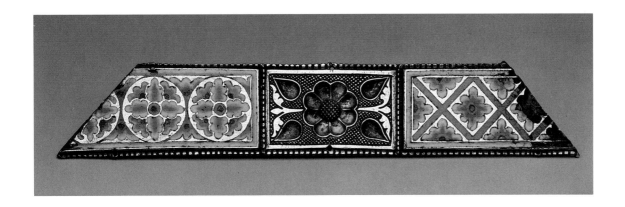

Fig. 17. Ornamental Plaques
Virginia Museum of Fine Arts, Richmond

9

ORNAMENTAL PLAQUE
Cologne, ca. 1160-1170
Champlevé enamel and gilding on copper
H: 93 mm. (3¹¹⁄₁₆ in.) W: 42 mm. (1¹¹⁄₁₆ in.)
47.1442   *Frederick Brown Fund*

PROVENANCE: von Nagler, Berlin; Königlich-Preussische Kunstkammer, Berlin; J. Rosenbaum, Frankfurt; Rosenberg and Stiebel, Inc., New York; Joseph Brummer, New York

BIBLIOGRAPHY: Verdier 1975, p. 26 n. 6

DESCRIPTION: Rectangular plaque with two beaded sides; three pinholes. Hammered, tooled, *champlevé*, enameled, and gilded. Enamel colors are lapis blue, light blue, turquoise (two shades), green (two shades), yellow, and white in single and mixed fields of up to three colors. Within a blue and white border, blue and white tendrils form three hearts, each separated by a pair of turquoise and white leaves. Springing from a green and white bud are a pair of tightly curled leaves at the bottom (blue and white inside and turquoise and white outside), a pair of leaves wrapping around the tendrils (turquoise and white inside and green and white outside), and a blue and white scalloped central stalk that sits below a green and white arch and a series of small yellow circles alternating with blue and white rectangles. The accession number "K4203c" of the Königlich-Preussische Kunstkammer is written in india ink on the reverse.

CONDITION: Rough upper and lower edges indicate that the plaque has been cut. The absence of leaves below the lowest heart reveals that only the border has been cut on the bottom. The enamel pattern may have continued, however, on the top. Pinholes are modern. Areas filled with plaster replace lost enamel near upper and lower edges.

This is one of four small plaques of the same design that were in the Königlich-Preussische Kunstkammer in Berlin.[1] All may have belonged to a single long plaque. The vertical emphasis of the design suggests that this example may have served as a pilaster on a large shrine. Although somewhat finer in execution and less schematized than the present example, two pilasters on the roof of Saint Heribert's Shrine in Deutz (ca. 1160-1170)[2] and two plaques forming the frame of the altar from the Church of Saint Ursula in Cologne (ca. 1170)[3] show a similar profile acanthus placed within heart-shaped tendrils.

1. Acc. nos. K4203a-d. The other three plaques have been lost since 1945. The authors are grateful to Dietrich Kötzsche for this information.

2. See Schnitzler 1959, pp. 32-34, no. 26, pl. 90; Cologne 1985, vol. 2, pp. 314-323, no. E91.

3. Schnütgen Museum, Cologne, acc. no. 6569. See Cologne 1985, vol. 2, p. 348, no. E113.

10

ORNAMENTAL PLAQUE
Rhineland or Meuse or North Germany, last
third of 12th century
Champlevé and *cloisonné* enamel and gilding on
copper
H: 15 mm. (¹⁰⁄₁₆ in.) W: 352 mm. (13⅞ in.)
43.216 *Seth K. Sweetser Fund*

PROVENANCE: R. von Passavant-Gontard, Frankfurt;
Harry Fuld, Frankfurt; Raphael Stora, New York

DESCRIPTION: Rectangular plaque, slightly curved
in the middle; pinholes on each end and in the center.
Hammered, *champlevé*, *cloisonné*, enameled, and gilded.
Enamel colors are lapis blue, turquoise, and white in
single fields. The decoration consists of opposing
white *cloisonné* trefoils on a lapis-blue ground within a
turquoise border; on the reverse are traces of an accession number in india ink.

CONDITION: Enamel is missing from the center and
there are smaller losses at the ends.

Long narrow strips with simple *cloisonné* patterns
are often found as borders on reliquaries. Those
on Charlemagne's arm reliquary, probably made
in Liège about 1166-1170,[1] and on a North
German portable altar in Berlin from the last
quarter of the twelfth century,[2] are closely related
to the present plaque. The quality, which is not
as high as that of other mixed *cloisonné* and
champlevé enamels (see nos. 17 and 19), indicates
routine production and makes the piece difficult
to localize and date precisely.

1. Musée du Louvre acc. no. D712. See Stuttgart
1977, no. 538, with bibliography.
2. Kunstgewerbemuseum acc. no. W14. See Kötzsche
1973a, p. 71, no. 14.

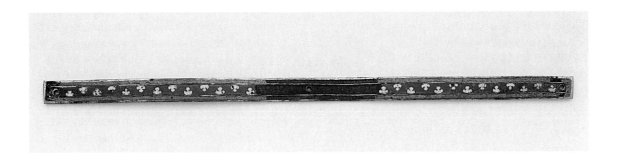

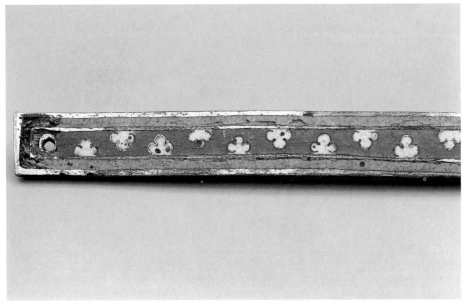

detail

· 11 ·

ORNAMENTAL LUNETTE

Rhineland or Meuse, ca. 1170
Champlevé enamel and gilding on copper
H: 24 mm. (1 in.) W: 49 mm. (1¹⁵⁄₁₆ in.)
50.820   *William E. Nickerson Fund*

PROVENANCE: Paul Garnier, Paris

BIBLIOGRAPHY: Cologne 1964a, no. 39

DESCRIPTION: Semicircular plaque with beaded border on arch; three pinholes. Hammered, tooled, *champlevé*, enameled, and gilded. Enamel colors are lapis blue, azure blue, turquoise, green, yellow, red, and white in single and mixed fields. A framing arch of turquoise and blue surrounds a tuft of leaves emerging from a red and white semicircular stem. Four pairs of leaves are arranged symmetrically around a central lapis-blue, azure-blue, and white stalk. From the center out, the first and fourth pairs are green and yellow. The second and third are turquoise and white inside and lapis blue and white outside. Two red and white scalloped triangles come between the second and third pairs of leaves. The accession number "384" is written in india ink on the reverse.

CONDITION: The plaque has been regilded, and there are losses of enamel, especially on the framing arch and lower and central leaves.

The lunette belongs with six of similar shape, size, and decoration in the Hessisches Landesmuseum, Darmstadt,[1] one of which is virtually identical. With related enamel decoration, but with molded edges and of slightly narrower width, a group of ten other lunettes (dispersed among the Cluny Museum,[2] the Louvre,[3] the Keir Collection,[4] and several private collections[5]) are probably products of the same workshop. Lunettes of this kind were used on shrines to mask joins of enamel frames;[6] they also form lobes of quatrefoils on phylacteries.[7]

Although coarser in execution, the lunettes'
flaccid, twisted leaves with scalloped edges resemble enamels on the lid of the arm reliquary of Charlemagne[8] and the shrines of Saint Maurinus (see note 6) and Saint Aetherius produced about 1170 in Cologne.[9] Two halos with related decoration are in the Keir Collection.[10] Other similar plaques, once together in the Königlich-Preussischen Kunstkammer in Berlin, were formerly divided between the Brummer and von Hirsch Collections.[11]

1. Acc. nos. Kg 54:241a-f. See Cologne 1964a, no. 39.

2. Acc. no. LOAR 357.

3. Acc. no. OA.10028.

4. See Schnitzler 1965, p. 17, no. E20.

5. Rütschi (sale, Galerie Fischer, Lucerne, September 5, 1931, nos. 48-51); Ernest Brummer, New York (sale, Galerie Koller, Zurich, October 16-19, 1979, nos. 200a-b); (sale, Sotheby, London, April 13, 1978, no. 15).

6. Compare, for example, the modern lunettes (presumably replacing originals) on the roof of the Shrine of Saint Maurinus in Saint Pantaleon in Cologne. See Schnitzler 1959, no. 27; Cologne 1985, vol. 2, pp. 296-300, no. E79.

7. For example, one in the Cleveland Museum of Art (acc. no. 26.428; see Gauthier 1972, p. 138, fig. 96) and another in the Treasury of the Cathedral of Namur (see H. Swarzenski 1954, fig. 426).

8. Musée du Louvre acc. no. D712. See Stuttgart 1977, no. 538, with bibliography.

9. See Von Falke and Frauberger 1904, pls. II-X; Cologne 1985, vol. 2, pp. 349-351, no. E114.

10. See Schnitzler 1965, pp. 17-18, nos. E17, E23.

11. Brummer (see note 5) nos. 203, 204, 205, 206, 215 (no. 203 is now in the Musée d'art religieux et d'art mosan in Liège; see Liège 1980, no. A12); Robert von Hirsch, Basel (sale, Sotheby Parke-Bernet, London, June 22, 1978, no. 220).

12

PAIR OF ORNAMENTAL PLAQUES
Rhineland or Meuse, last quarter of 12th century
Champlevé enamel and gilding on copper
H: 68 mm. (2¹¹⁄₁₆ in.) W: 22 mm. (⅞ in.)
50.821a-b   *William E. Nickerson Fund*

PROVENANCE: Paul Garnier, Paris

DESCRIPTION: Rectangular plaques beaded on the long sides; two pinholes on each. Hammered, tooled, *champlevé*, enameled, and gilded. Enamel colors are lapis blue, turquoise, green, yellow, red, and white in single and mixed fields of up to three colors. Within a lapis-blue border on three sides, lozenges composed of two strands (one turquoise and white and the other lapis blue and white) contain lapis-blue rosettes with white edges and blue centers. Triangular spaces are filled with demi-rosettes in green with yellow edges and red centers. On the reverse of *a* is a zigzag design (possibly chisel trials or assembly marks).

CONDITION: Short edges, where the border is missing, have modern cuts, indicating that the two originally formed a single plaque. There are minor losses of enamel around the edges.

The two plaques once framed a Carolingian ivory in the Museum's collection.[1] Their lozenge-and-rosette motif is one of the most common in Mosan and Rhenish enamelwork and therefore makes the present pieces difficult to localize and date precisely. Closest in design and execution to these plaques is a slightly wider one in the Keir Collection.[2] Another, higher in quality, is a curved plaque on the central arch of the Shrine of Saint Aetherius made in Cologne about 1170.[3]

1. Acc. no. 50.819. (See H. Swarzenski 1952, pp. 2-7, esp. fig. 8.) The frame also included no. 11.

2. See Schnitzler 1965, p. 16, no. E16.

3. In Saint Ursula, Cologne. See von Falke and Frauberger 1904, pl. V; Cologne 1985, vol. 2, pp. 349-351, no. E114.

13

PLAQUE WITH HEAD IN MEDALLION
Cologne, ca. 1183
Champlevé enamel and gilding on copper
H: 27 mm. (1¹⁄₁₆ in.) W: 27 mm. (1¹⁄₁₆ in.)
1974.535 *Seth K. Sweetser Fund*

PROVENANCE: Shrine of Saint Anno, Saint Michael's Abbey, Siegburg; Paul Beumers, Düsseldorf; Geladakis, Paris; Joseph Brummer, New York; Georg Swarzenski, Boston

BIBLIOGRAPHY: Kötzsche 1973a, p. 224; Verdier 1975, p. 78 n. 3

EXHIBITIONS: Boston 1940, no. 251

DESCRIPTION: Lozenge plaque with four pinholes. Hammered, *champlevé*, enameled, and gilded. Enamel color is lapis blue. Trilobed gilded leaves in relief fill the corners around a medallion with a frontal head in reserve against a lapis-blue ground.

CONDITION: Enamel is missing above the head.

Mounted on the frames of the lost reliefs on the roof of the Shrine of Saint Anno, produced in Cologne about 1183,[1] are fifty-four similar enamels with frontal heads. Like the Boston plaque, several have slightly oblique noses, centrally parted long hair, eyes cast to one side, and a heavy contour line marking the chin. At least ten of the Anno plaques, those marked "C.A.B. 1902," were made by Paul Beumers when he restored the shrine between 1901 and 1902. The present damaged plaque (and perhaps one in the Musée des Beaux-Arts in Niort,[2] another belonging to Wolfgang Swarzenski,[3] and three others in the Walters Art Gallery in Baltimore[4]) was probably removed by Beumers at the time of his restoration.[5]

The heads are clearly inspired by antique models, and similar painted heads decorate the frames of early medieval miniatures.[6] A nearly identical head surrounded by four trefoil leaves is found in the initial O in a contemporary Rhenish manuscript in Mainz.[7] The Anno heads are also partic-

ularly close to that on a square fibula with *cloisonné* enamel in Laon.[8]

The use of classical heads on the Anno Shrine is in keeping with the twelfth-century practice of adorning shrines and liturgical objects with antique gems and cameos. The practice continued with a series of similar heads in *vernis brun* applied to the roof of the Shrine of the Three Kings in Cologne Cathedral[9] and a row of three-quarter heads engraved in square plaques on the socles of Saint Elizabeth's Shrine at Marburg.[10]

1. Now in Saint Michael's Abbey, Siegburg. (See Cologne 1975, pp. 185-205, esp. pp. 202-205; Zehender 1967, pp. 388-400; Schnitzler 1959, pp. 44-46, no. 37; Cologne 1985, vol. 2, pp. 457-458, no. F90.) Originally there were fifty-six heads on the shrine. Those under the central finial are missing on both sides.
2. Acc. no. 324 (gift of M. Piet-Lataudrie in 1909).
3. Formerly Joseph Brummer, New York.
4. Acc. nos. 44.603-605. (Formerly Joseph Brummer, New York [sale, Parke-Bernet, April 23, 1949, no. 697, ill. p. 183].) See New York 1970, p. 179, no. 184.
5. Technical analyses suggest no reason to doubt the authenticity of this plaque.
6. See Mütherich 1941, pp. 60-61; Cologne 1975, p. 197.
7. Stadtbibliothek MS II.53 f. 43v. See G. Swarzenski and Schilling 1929, p. 11.
8. Musée Municipal. The fibula was excavated at Chalandry in an archaeological stratum assigned to the fourth century, but some have thought it could be contemporary with the Anno plaques. See Rosenberg 1922, pp. 1-2, fig. 1; Gauthier 1972, pp. 25, 315; Cologne 1975, pp. 197-198, 202; and, for the controversy over its date, Gauthier 1979, p. 79.
9. See Cologne 1964b, pp. 15-18; Schnitzler 1959, no. 29; Cologne 1985, vol. 2, pp. 216-224, no. E18.
10. See Dinkler-von Schubert 1964, pl. 57, figs. 185-186.

14

HALO
Cologne, ca. 1183
Champlevé enamel and gilding on copper
DIAM: 68 mm. (2¹¹⁄₁₆ in.)
47.1443   *1941 Purchase Fund*

PROVENANCE: Shrine of Saint Anno, Saint Michael's Abbey, Siegburg (?); Saint Servatius, Siegburg (?); Paul Beumers, Düsseldorf; Geladakis, Paris; Joseph Brummer, New York

DESCRIPTION: Circular plaque with beaded edge (arch cut from bottom); three pinholes. Hammered, tooled, *champlevé*, enameled, and gilded. Enamel colors are lapis blue (two shades), turquoise (two shades), green (two shades), white, yellow, and pale mauve in mixed fields of up to three colors. A large schematized blossom against gold ground emanates from the blue and white border. Four large curled leaves with scalloped borders are two shades of lapis blue with white edges. Those on the bottom contain berries in two shades of green. The same shades and yellow are used for the four flat scalloped leaves. Pointed leaves in the center are two shades of turquoise and all but the one at the bottom have a blue center. The central arch and two pointed leaves on the top are light mauve. On the reverse are an engraved hand with extended finger, a grid pattern,[1] and assembly marks "EVI III" (the latter may be modern).

CONDITION: The halo has probably been regilded and there are carbon particles in the enamel.

An enamel identical to the present one belongs to a group of halos preserved since the nineteenth century in the Treasury of Saint Servatius in Siegburg.[2] The Boston halo may also have been among them before it came to Paul Beumers, probably when he restored several of the shrines in the Treasury about the turn of the century.[3] These two halos and others in the Trea-sury group (of similar size and with related designs) probably come from the same source.

The complex symmetrical blossoms with a combination of curled and flat scalloped leaves are related to those on the rectangular plaques and finials of the Anno Shrine, made in Cologne about 1183 (see no. 13).[4] The design and quality of the halos suggest that they could have belonged to the seated bishop saints on the long sides of that shrine. These figures, which were removed between 1803 and 1812 (just before the shrine was moved to Saint Servatius, where it remained until 1955), are shown with decorative halos in a remarkably accurate painting of the shrine from 1764 in the Parish Church at Belecke.[5]

1. For this mark (reversed) see Rosenberg 1928, vol. 3, p. 309, no. 4541.

2. One of the two identical halos is reproduced in a drawing in Aus'm Weerth 1866, vol. 1, pt. 3, pl. XLIV, 3. The Siegburg halo has been reused with others from the group on the front of a cross made by Joseph Jaeckel in 1953; some of the other halos are reused on a modern tabernacle made in 1959. See Zehender 1967, no. 12, pp. 450-453, pls. 195-196.

3. Technical analyses of the halo suggest no reason to doubt the authenticity of the Boston piece. It would be useful to examine the Siegburg halo to determine its authenticity.

4. See Von Falke and Frauberger 1904, pls. XIV, XVI; Schnitzler 1959, no. 37; Cologne 1985, vol. 2, pp. 457-458, no. F90. See also no. 13.

5. See Cologne 1975, pp. 185-193. A halo in the Museum für Kunstgewerbe in Hamburg (acc. no. 1890.133), similar in decoration to others preserved in the Siegburg Treasury, is also said to have come from the Anno Shrine.

PLAQUE WITH BEASTS
Cologne, ca. 1185
Champlevé enamel and gilding on copper
H: 30 mm. (1¾₆ in.) W: 87 mm. (3⁷₁₆ in.)
47.1445   *Otis Norcross Fund*

PROVENANCE: Shrine of Saints Mauritius and Innocentius in Saint Servatius, Siegburg; Paul Beumers, Düsseldorf; Geladakis, Paris; Joseph Brummer, New York

BIBLIOGRAPHY: *Boston Museum Bulletin* 1957, p. 79, no. 30; Cologne 1964a, no. 44

DESCRIPTION: Rectangular plaque with beaded edges; six pinholes. Hammered, tooled, *champlevé*, enameled, and gilded. Enamel colors are lapis blue, turquoise, and light blue in single and mixed fields of two colors. Three lapis-blue rectangles depict a fantastic beast in reserve, engraved and filled with lapis-blue enamel. Rectangles are framed by a reserve band and two turquoise and light-blue enamel bands. Two dog-like beasts crouch facing toward the center with noses to the ground and long tails tucked under their bodies. The central beast, resembling a ram, faces right. On the reverse the number "14" is written in india ink.

CONDITION: There are minute losses of enamel.

Plaques of similar size and precision (also divided into three or four blue fields, each containing a beast in reserve) decorate the cornice of the Shrine of Saints Mauritius and Innocentius, made in Cologne about 1185.[1] As technical analyses reveal no reason for questioning the authenticity of the piece, it may be assumed that the Boston plaque was removed from the shrine during its restoration in 1902 by Paul Beumers, from whose collection it comes. A plaque very similar to the present one on the shrine's front gable may be his replacement. Two others in the Metropolitan Museum in New York,[2] showing dragons and eagles in a related style and reused in a mid-nineteenth-century pastiche, must have been removed earlier from the shrine.

1. In Saint Servatius, Siegburg. See Cologne 1975, pp. 207-210; Zehender 1967, pp. 400-407.
2. Acc. nos. 17.190.2142-2143 (see New York 1970, no. 189, p. 183). The plaques were mounted on a triptych made by Alexis Berg in Paris in 1854 (see Kötzsche 1973a, p. 221).

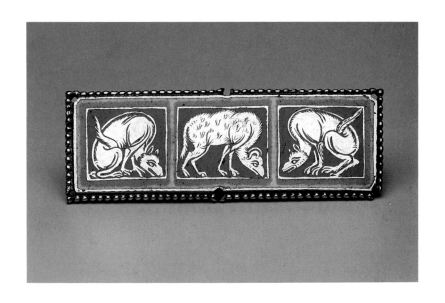

16

Four Ornamental Colonnettes
Cologne, ca. 1185
Champlevé enamel and gilding on copper
(shafts); gilding on brass (capitals and bases)
H: 250 mm. (9¹³⁄₁₆ in.)
68.554a-d   *Edwin E. Jack Fund*

PROVENANCE: Shrine of Saints Mauritius and Innocentius in Saint Servatius, Siegburg (?); Duchess of
Mecklenburg, Burg Rheinstein near Bingen

BIBLIOGRAPHY: *Boston Museum Annual Report* 1968,
ill. p. 38

DESCRIPTION: Separate capitals, shafts, and bases
with assembly marks. Capitals and bases are cast,
chased, and gilded. Shafts are hammered, *champlevé*,
curved, enameled, and gilded. Enamel colors are lapis
blue, light blue, turquoise, yellow, and white. The gilt-
brass *ajouré* capitals, open in back, show an eagle with
spread wings on three sides. Eagles and abaci are
chased with geometric patterns. Bases are a simple
baluster type. Colonnette *a* has alternating bands of
lapis-blue borders containing turquoise lozenges with
yellow quatrefoils and small turquoise squares with
gilded quatrefoils against a light-blue ground. Colonnette *b* has a lapis-blue trellis around turquoise lozenges with white quatrefoils. On colonnette *c*, a spiral
pattern of lapis-blue lozenges with white quatrefoils
alternates with white lozenges filled with lapis-blue
quatrefoils. The trellis consists of alternating turquoise,
lapis-blue, and white segments. Colonnette *d* has a
lapis-blue trellis enclosing white lozenges with lapis-
blue quatrefoils. When purchased, the colonnettes
were displayed on a neo-Gothic wooden shrine.

CONDITION: File marks on both sides of the abaci
and plinths adjacent to the back corners suggest
removal of attachment loops. Traces of adhesive in oval
cavities on the abacus of colonnette *d* indicate that
fillings (probably glass paste) are missing. One eagle
head on colonnette *b* is broken. The capital of colonnette *d* is cracked on the left side. There are small losses
of enamel on all shafts, and the gilding on colonnette *d*
is abraded on the left side. The bases were filled with
epoxy just after they came to the Museum.

Colonnettes of this type usually support arcades
on reliquary shrines, many of which were made
in Cologne during the late twelfth and early
thirteenth century. The size, enamel designs,
capitals, bases, and assembly marks of the present
examples match those of four colonnettes in the
Metropolitan Museum in New York,[1] two in

the Hermitage in Leningrad,[2] one in the Walters
Art Gallery in Baltimore,[3] and another recently
sold in Paris.[4] (The Metropolitan also has an
identical eagle capital, presumably from another
colonnette.[5]) Although slightly smaller and with
capitals showing palmettes flanked by acanthus,
two colonnettes in the Abegg Collection in Riggisberg,[6] another in the Walters,[7] and one in the
Detroit Institute[8] have bases, decoration, and
assembly marks revealing that they come from
the same shrine as the others.

The two types of capitals are found together
on a shrine in the Germeau Collection known
only from a photograph and a published engraving of 1870,[9] by which time the shrine had disappeared. The Germeau shrine appears to be a
nineteenth-century pastiche decorated with
assorted *spolia* of the twelfth and thirteenth centuries. The Detroit and Walters colonnettes with
acanthus capitals (said to have come from the
Germeau Collection) match those in the center
of the photograph. The colonnette with the eagle
capital on the left is the one recently sold in
Paris; that on the right may be one of those in
the Hermitage (its nineteenth-century provenance unfortunately is unknown). The remaining
Walters and Abegg colonnettes, which also
belonged to Germeau, were probably on one of
the other sides.

Localization and dating of these sixteen colonnettes and the single capital to a Cologne workshop about 1185 are based on their similarity to
the colonnettes of comparable size, eagle capitals,
and enamel designs on the Shrine of Saints Mauritius and Innocentius in the Church of Saint
Servatius in Siegburg.[10] They may, in fact, be
elements original to it; four of the colonnettes on
the shrine – marked "C.A.B. 1902" or "C.A.
Beumers, Düsseldorf 1902" – are certainly
replacements[11] and there is reason to suspect that
others are replacements as well.

1. Acc. nos. 41.100.143-146. (Formerly G. Stroganoff,
Rome; Daguerre, Paris; Arnold Seligman, Paris;
G. Blumenthal, Paris.) See Muñoz 1911, p. 214.
2. Acc. nos. 1457, 1458. (Before 1904, G. Stroganoff,
Rome; until 1919, Museum of the Society for the

Encouragement of Arts, Leningrad.) See Lapkovskaya 1971, pp. 5-6; Lafontaine-Dosogne 1975, pp. 104-105.

3. Acc. no. 44.597. (Formerly J. Brummer, New York [sale, Parke-Bernet, New York, April 23, 1949, nos. 717-718].) See New York 1970, pp. 181-182, no. 187.

4. Sales, Hôtel Drouot, Paris, March 23, 1985, no. 36; and Parke-Bernet, New York, April 23, 1949, no. 734.

5. Acc. no. 17.190.415. See Peraté 1911, no. 24, pl. 11.

6. Acc. nos. 8.53.63; 8.54.63. See Stettler and Otavsky 1973, pl. 29.

7. Acc. no. 44.598 (see note 3).

8. Acc. no. 49.349. (Formerly M. Germeau, Paris; Dereppe, Paris; A. Seligman, Paris; J. Brummer, New York [sale, Parke-Bernet, May 14, 1949, nos. 730, 732].) See *Detroit Bulletin* 1951, p. 74.

9. See *Encyclopédie* 1870, p. 2204; Otavsky 1973, pp. 51-55.

10. See Cologne 1975, pp. 207-210; Zehender 1967, pp. 400-407. See also no. 15.

11. See Zehender 1967, p. 405.

17

ORNAMENTAL PLAQUE
Cologne, ca. 1186
Champlevé and *cloisonné* enamel and gilding on
copper
H: 29 mm. (1³⁄₁₆ in.) W: 156 mm. (6⅛ in.)
47.1444   *William E. Nickerson Fund*

PROVENANCE: Shrine of Saint Albinus in Saint
Pantaleon, Cologne; Paul Beumers, Düsseldorf;
Geladakis, Paris; Joseph Brummer, New York

DESCRIPTION: Rectangular plaque with six pinholes.
Hammered, *champlevé*, *cloisonné*, enameled, and gilded.
Enamel colors are lapis blue, turquoise, red, and white
in single and mixed fields. An imbrication pattern
consists of two rows of semicircles filled with trilobed
cloisonné leaves and triangular centers. The bottom row
alternates between red grounds with white leaves and
turquoise triangles and white grounds with red leaves
and red triangles. Blue grounds, white leaves, and a
mixed center field of red and turquoise fill the upper
row. Spandrels on the top are alternately turquoise
with single red *cloisonné* leaves and red with white
leaves. On the reverse are two sets of zigzag bands
(possibly assembly marks or chisel trials).

CONDITION: There are minor losses of enamel in
some leaves.

This plaque is related to one in the Metropolitan
Museum (fig. 18) that has medallions also containing trilobed *cloisonné* leaves.[1] Both are virtually identical to ones framing the roof reliefs on
the shrine of Saint Albinus made in Cologne
about 1186.[2] On this shrine two identical
enamels are often placed side by side, separated

by small square gilded plaques. The Boston and
Metropolitan enamels may well have been
arranged with their counterparts in this manner
before the shrine suffered considerable losses and
damage during the early nineteenth century.[3] A
photograph published in 1904[4] indicates that the
present plaques were then missing. How and
when they came into the hands of the restorer
Paul Beumers[5] is unknown.

The combination of *champlevé* with *cloisonné*
leaves occurs frequently on Rhenish enamels of
the last quarter of the twelfth century, as does the
imbricated circle pattern. Comparable, if more
intricate, designs are found on enamels on the
Shrine of the Three Kings in Cologne
Cathedral.[6]

1. Acc. no. 52.76.3. (Formerly Paul Beumers, Düsseldorf; Geladakis, Paris; Joseph Brummer, New York
[sale, Parke-Bernet, May 14, 1949, no. 721]; Alastair
Martin, Glen Head, New York.)
2. In Saint Pantaleon, Cologne. See Schnitzler 1959,
pp. 35-36, no. 28, pls. 101-103; Cologne 1985, vol. 2,
pp. 298-303, no. E80.
3. On restorations, see Kesseler 1951, pp. 41-45.
4. See Von Falke and Frauberger 1904, pl. 53.
5. There is no record of his having worked on the
shrine, which was restored by Karl Kesseler in 1949-
1950. Technical analyses of the Boston plaque indicate
no reason for doubting its authenticity.
6. See Schnitzler 1959, pp. 36-40, no. 29; Cologne
1985, vol. 2, pp. 216-224, no. E18.

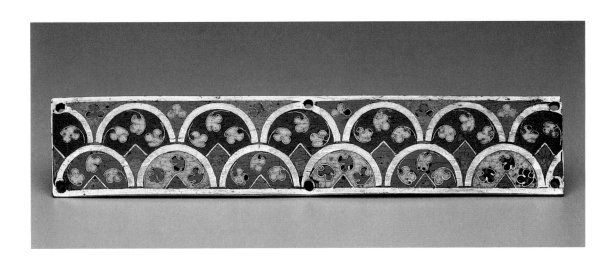

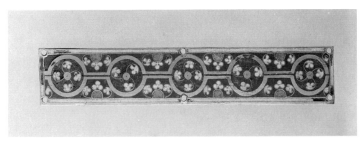

Fig. 18. Ornamental Plaque.
Metropolitan Museum of Art, New York

18

ORNAMENTAL PLAQUE
Cologne, ca. 1181-1200
Vernis brun and gilding on copper
H: 48 mm. (1⅞ in.) W: 29 mm. (1³⁄₁₆ in.)
52.1083   *Gift of John Hunt*

PROVENANCE: Julius Goldschmidt, London; John Hunt, Dublin

BIBLIOGRAPHY: Schilling 1950, p. 84, fig. 4

DESCRIPTION: Rectangular plaque with four pinholes in corners and minute beading on bottom edge. Hammered, engraved, fired, scraped, and gilded. Two acanthus scrolls and part of a third are shown against a gold ground. A narrow brown border surrounds the design on three sides.

CONDITION: The missing border and the ragged edge on one short side indicate that the plaque has been cut. Gilding is abraded on the edges.

This is one of at least five *vernis brun* plaques that – along with other late-twelfth-century enamels, filigree plaques, and glass-paste cameos – once decorated the top of a modern casket. In the 1940s, the casket was dismantled and the applied pieces were dispersed among various collections.[1] The present plaque and another (fig. 19) are in the Museum of Fine Arts in Boston,[2] two are in the Virginia Museum of Fine Arts in Richmond (fig. 20a and b),[3] and the location of the fifth is unknown.[4] Technical analysis reveals that three plaques – the present one and the two in Richmond – were made according to the traditional medieval method described by the monk Theophilus in the twelfth century,[5] i.e., by etching the design lightly on the copper plate, applying linseed oil, firing, and then scraping the burnt oil away from the areas to be gilded. The five plaques were cut from longer strips and their short ends are all approximately the same length. The Boston example and one in Richmond with the same acanthus scrolls (fig. 20b) are the ends of two separate pieces. The plaque whose present location is unknown has the same scrolls and appears to be the other end of the strip to which the Richmond plaque belongs. The second Richmond plaque (fig. 20a), decorated with profile acanthus, comes from yet another strip. With the same profile acanthus, the other plaque in Boston (fig. 19) appears to be modern. It is somewhat higher than the rest, has borders on all sides and modern pinholes, and, most important, approximates the true *vernis brun* with its brown fields cut into the copper as in *champlevé*. Furthermore, the dimensions of its profile acanthus, identical to those on the Richmond plaque (fig. 20a), indicate that its design may have been traced from that object.

It has been suggested that most of the applied pieces on the modern casket were removed in the nineteenth century from the Shrine of the Three Kings, made in Cologne about 1181-1200[6]; the acanthus scrolls are compared to those on wider plaques placed behind double columns on the shrine.[7] Although the designs are indeed similar, the present group lacks the precision of those on the shrine and probably comes from a different contemporary source.

1. See Schilling 1950, pp. 81-84.

2. Acc. no. 52.1082.

3. Acc. nos. 68.59.1-2. See Verdier 1974, fig. 20.

4. See Schilling 1950, p. 84, fig. 4.

5. See Dodwell 1961, pp. 147-148. We are grateful to Pinckney Near for lending his objects to the research laboratory for examination.

6. In Cologne Cathedral. See Schnitzler 1959, pp. 36-40, no. 29; Cologne 1985, vol. 2, pp. 216-224, no. E18.

7. See Schilling 1950, p. 84; Schnitzler 1959, pls. 114-115.

Fig. 19. Modern Plaque.
Museum of Fine Arts, Boston

Fig. 20a. Ornamental Plaque.
Virginia Museum of Fine Arts, Richmond

Fig. 20b. Ornamental Plaque.
Virginia Museum of Fine Arts, Richmond

19

ORNAMENTAL PLAQUE
Cologne, late 12th–early 13th century
Champlevé and *cloisonné* enamel and gilding on copper
H: 36 mm. (1 7/16 in.) W: 103 mm. (5⅛ in.) D: 7 mm. (¼ in.)
52.1084   *Gift of Alastair B. Martin*

PROVENANCE: Alastair Martin, Glen Head, New York

DESCRIPTION: Obtuse-angled plaque with molded and beaded edge (a triangular cut in the lower edge); seven pinholes in the angles and through the outer left quatrefoil. Hammered, tooled, *champlevé*, *cloisonné*, enameled, and gilded. Enamel colors are lapis blue, light blue, green, yellow, red, and white in fields of one or two colors. Within a lapis-blue and green border, a light-blue field contains four lapis-blue quatrefoils flanking a trefoil of the same color. Quatrefoils are filled with white *cloisonné* crossflowers with red centers. In the trefoil, three white *cloisonné* rosettes with red centers surround a yellow circle. Yellow scalloped semicircles with red centers in *cloisonné* are placed along the border. On the reverse is the modern assembly mark "VI."

CONDITION: There are minor losses of enamel, primarily around pinholes.

Identical in size, shape, and fastening holes is a plaque with a related enamel design in the collection of Ella Brummer in New York.[1] Both probably formed the pinnacle of a pointed arch on the side of a shrine. Their decoration with trefoils and quatrefoils and a combination of *champlevé* and *cloisonné* relate them to the enamels framing arches on the Klosterneuberg Altar of Nicholas of Verdun (completed in 1181)[2] and on the Shrine of the Three Kings in Cologne Cathedral, made between about 1181 and the early thirteenth century.[3] Several other plaques of similar design – reused in the nineteenth century on a book cover in the collection of the Duke of Arenberg in Brussels,[4] a casket,[5] and a cross[6] – probably come from the same workshop.

1. Sale, Galerie Koller, Zurich, October 16-19, 1979, no. 220, ill. The piece remains in the Brummer collection.

2. See Röhrig 1955 and Buschhausen 1980.

3. See Schnitzler 1959, pp. 36-40, no. 29; Cologne 1985, vol. 2, pp. 216-224, no. E18.

4. The manuscript is now Morgan Library M869, but the enamels from the binding were sold to Germain Seligmann in 1955. Some of these plaques are in the Metropolitan Museum in New York (acc. nos. 69.238.1-3); the Keir Collection in Kansas City (see Schnitzler 1965, pp. 16-18; nos. E15, 18, 19, 21, 24, 25; pl. 34; Stokstad 1983, no. 8); the Menil Foundation in Houston (acc. no. 7809. DJ; see New York 1970. p. 185, no. 191); and the Cleveland Museum (acc. no. 53.275; see New York 1970, p. 181, no. 186).

5. For this casket, dismantled in the 1940s by a London dealer, see no. 18 and Schilling (1950, pp. 81-84, fig. 2), who believes these plaques come from the Shrine of the Three Kings. The plaques are now in the Victoria and Albert Museum in London (acc. nos. M476-484.1956).

6. See Schilling 1950, p. 84, fig. 1. The plaques are now in the Bayerisches Nationalmuseum in Munich (acc. no. 229).

20

PLAQUE WITH BUSTS OF FOUR ANGELS
Cologne, ca. 1220-1230
Champlevé enamel and gilding on copper
H: 29 mm. (1⅛ in.) W: 133 mm. (5¼ in.)
41.218 *Harriet Otis Cruft Fund*

PROVENANCE: Joseph Brummer, New York; Arnold Seligmann Rey and Company, New York

BIBLIOGRAPHY: Cologne 1964a, no. 44

DESCRIPTION: Rectangular plaque with four pinholes. Hammered, *champlevé*, enameled, and gilded. Enamel colors are lapis blue, red, white, and green in single and mixed fields of three colors. Four red arches contain busts of angels in reserve against a lapis-blue ground. The angels are arranged in facing pairs. Between the arches and under smaller scalloped arches in reserve are fields of white, blue, and green enamel. Rough crosshatching in blue enamel fills the space between the arches and the upper border. On the reverse are two sets of zigzag bands (chisel trials or assembly marks) at each end and an accession number, "966," in white over india ink.

CONDITION: There are large losses of enamel in the lapis-blue fields and red arches and smaller losses of enamel in the spandrels. Two pinholes on the left have been enlarged.

This plaque belongs with at least twenty-one of similar size, quality, and color, in which designs with enamel arches, triangles, medallions, or lozenges are filled with busts of angels, beasts, or rosettes. There are four in the Hessisches Landesmuseum in Darmstadt,[1] one in the Kunstgewerbemuseum in Cologne,[2] one in the Schnütgen Museum in Cologne,[3] one in a private collection in Munich,[4] and two in the Louvre in Paris.[5] Four plaques in the Cluny Museum in Paris[6] and eight in the Fitzwilliam Museum in Cambridge[7] were reused in the nineteenth century on the covers of illuminated manuscripts. Their designs are similar to those of several plaques on the Cologne Shrine of Saint Albinus from about 1186,[8] but the very sketchy rendering of the figures and beasts relates them more closely to enamels on two arm reliquaries from Saint Gereon in Cologne, usually dated 1220-1230.[9] The plaques were probably removed from a reliquary in the nineteenth century.

1. Acc. nos. Kg 54.244a-b; Kg 54.245a-b. See Degen 1955, pp. 3, 32-33, ill. p. 42; Cologne 1964a, nos. 43-44.

2. Acc. no. G712. See Cologne 1981, p. 52, no. 22.

3. Acc. no. 6539.

4. See Cologne 1964a, no. 44.

5. MR. 2668-2669. See Darcel 1891, nos. 79-80.

6. Acc. no. 1250.

7. MS McClean 75. See Dalton 1912, no. 56.

8. In Saint Pantaleon, Cologne. See Von Falke and Frauberger 1904, pl. XXI; Schnitzler 1959, pp. 35-36, no. 28, pls. 101-103; Cologne 1985, vol. 2, pp. 298-303, no. E80.

9. See Cologne 1985, vol. 2, pp. 242-245, nos. E35-36.

21

PLAQUE WITH TWO APOSTLES IN
MEDALLIONS
North Germany, last quarter of 12th century
Champlevé enamel and gilding on copper
H: 52 mm. (2⅛ in.) W: 97 mm. (3¹³⁄₁₆ in.)
43.217   *Seth K. Sweetser Fund*

PROVENANCE: R. von Passavant-Gontard, Frankfurt;
Harry Fuld, Frankfurt; Raphael Stora, New York

DESCRIPTION: Rectangular plaque with six pinholes.
Hammered, *champlevé*, enameled, and gilded. Enamel
colors are lapis blue, green, and red in single fields.
Two facing Apostles with centrally parted long hair,
one bearded and the other clean shaven, are placed
against a lapis-blue ground in medallions with green
borders. Each has a green halo and holds a green book.
Figures are in reserve with details engraved and filled
with red enamel. The background is lapis blue. A
vertical zigzag band (possibly an assembly mark or
chisel trial) appears on the reverse.

CONDITION: There are major losses of enamel, and
gilding is abraded.

The plaque, attached to a wooden core, probably
formed one of the short sides of a portable altar.

Several North German altars with Apostle busts
arranged in pairs are preserved; two Apostles
appear on the short sides and four are shown on
the long sides.[1] The placement of the busts in
medallions on the Boston plaque, however,
appears to be unique; others show Apostles
below arches or in rectangular spaces divided by
pilasters.

Although few North German enamels can be
assigned to specific centers, they do fall into
stylistic groups. Nearly identical in style and
undoubtedly from the same workshop is a portable altar in the Musée Cinquantenaire in Brussels.[2] Long narrow faces with round eyes and
parallel lines indicating drapery folds set these
two examples apart from others.

1. See von Falke and Frauberger 1904, pp. 114-115,
figs. 43, 45-47; Kötzsche 1973a, p. 71, no. 14.
2. Acc. no. 378. See Jansen 1964, no. 40, where it is
incorrectly called Limoges.

22

PENDANT
Limoges or Limoges workshop in England, late
12th century
Champlevé enamel and gilding on copper
DIAM.: 46 mm. (1³⁄₁₆ in.)
57.673 *Gift of Mr. and Mrs. John Hunt in honor
of Dr. Georg Swarzenski*

PROVENANCE: John Hunt, Dublin

BIBLIOGRAPHY: Cahn 1967, p. 381, pl. 309;
Gauthier 1985, no. 144

DESCRIPTION: An openwork roundel with beaded
border and suspension ring. *Repoussé, champlevé,*
punched, engraved, chased, cut out, enameled, and
gilded. An openwork dragon bends back to bite his
coiling tail, which terminates in large blossoms. The
dragon's wing, with *rinceaux* in reserve, was blue
enamel.

CONDITION: The gilding is almost completely
abraded. The lower right segment of the border is a
modern replacement, and only traces of blue enamel
remain on the wing.

Probably made for suspension from a horse har-
ness, the pendant is one of several Romanesque
examples[1] of a type that has been known since
antiquity.[2] Another of identical size and similar
openwork design, but badly corroded, was excavated at the end of the nineteenth century near
Thurso, Scotland.[3] It seems to belong to the
same series as the Boston pendant.

Openwork interlaced dragons with flowering
tails are common in late-twelfth- and thirteenth-
century Limoges metalwork. Particularly close in
design to the Boston pendant are the bosses
mounted on the cover of the Souvigny Bible in
Moulins[4] and four similar roundels, two now in
the Victoria and Albert Museum in London[5] and
two mounted on a manuscript cover in
Paderborn,[6] wherein the dragons also have enameled wings. Such comparisons indicate that the
present piece is the work of craftsmen trained in
the Limoges tradition. The fleshy floral blossoms
with edges curling in opposite directions, however, are closer to those in English manuscripts[7]
and metalwork of the twelfth century.[8] Thus, the
roundel may have been made in a Limoges workshop in England.[9] The excavation in Scotland of
the related pendant certainly supports such an
origin.

1. See the pendant formerly in the Adolphe Stocklet
collection (sale, Sotheby & Co., April 27, 1965, no.
39); one in the Salisbury and South Wiltshire Museum
(acc. no. 1/1923. OS.C.64; London 1984, p. 278, no.
295.); and one in the Germanisches Nationalmuseum
in Nüremberg (acc. no. KG1.34; Stuttgart 1977, p.
477, no. 601).
2. See, for example, the Barberini ivory in the Musée
du Louvre, Paris (acc. no. OA 9063; Volbach 1976, pp.
47-48, no. 48).
3. British Museum, London, acc. no. MLA 1985, 2-1,1.
The authors are grateful to Neil Stratford for bringing
this object to their attention.
4. See Cahn 1967, pp. 376-384; Gauthier 1981, pp.
141-153.
5. Acc. nos. 5.028-1.857 and M 577-1.910. See Mallé
1950, pp. 106-107; Cologne 1985, vol. I, p. 342,
B118-119.
6. Diözesanmuseum, Paderborn, acc. no. Pr52. See
Cologne 1985, vol. I, pp. 340-341, no. B117.
7. See Kauffmann 1975, pls. 122, 153, and 231.
8. See the crosier from the Cathedral of Saint David's;
London 1984, p. 257, no. 268a.
9. For other enamels, possibly of similar origin, see
ibid., pp. 276, 278, nos. 291, 293, and 294.

23

RELIEF OF CHRIST
Limoges, ca. 1210
Champlevé enamel and gilding on copper
H: 183 mm. (7³⁄₁₆ in.) W: 155 mm. (6⅛ in.)
D: 21 mm. (¹³⁄₁₆ in.)
49.472 *William Francis Warden Fund*

PROVENANCE: Robert Woods Bliss, Washington, D.C.; Joseph Brummer, New York (sale, Parke-Bernet, April 23, 1949, no. 712a)

DESCRIPTION: Frontal crucified Christ wearing a dalmatic and alb. A single copper sheet, cut out, *repoussé* (into a mold), *champlevé*, engraved, chased, enameled, and gilded. There is one pinhole in each hand. The eyes are dark-blue glass; the crown, inset with small beads of the same blue glass, is separate. The hole in the center of the belt probably held a cabochon. Enamel colors are lapis blue, green, red, and yellow in single and mixed fields of two colors. Christ's centrally parted wavy hair falls over the shoulder. Only the bottom of the alb (green with red dots) and its gilded cuffs, engraved to show folds, are visible below the lapis-blue dalmatic, which falls in two vertical rows of V-shaped folds, marked in reserve. It has a tied belt engraved with a simple wave pattern that continues down the front in two bands. The collar is green with circular and lozenge-shaped areas of red and yellow simulating gems.

CONDITION: The fingers of the left hand are broken off, and its pinhole is modern. The thumb of the right hand has been broken off. The feet, which were separate, are now missing, as are some beads from the crown and belt. There are losses of enamel, especially on the upper part of the garment, and the gilding is considerably abraded.

Crowned and clothed crucifixes belong to a rare type mounted on the main sides of processional crosses produced in Limoges in the early thirteenth century. Only three such crosses are still intact – those in Stockholm,[1] Baltimore,[2] and Vich[3] – but single figures of the same type are preserved in London,[4] Barcelona,[5] Oxford,[6] Leningrad,[7] Amiens,[8] Kansas City,[9] and the Louvre[10] and Cluny[11] museums in Paris. At least three others – those formerly in Berlin,[12] Montlevon,[13] and in the Villarmois collection[14] – are known from reproductions.

The Boston and Vich crucifixes are strictly frontal, while the others have slightly turned or inclined heads. The present relief is most closely related to that in Oxford. They are smaller, less elaborate, and probably later in date than those in Paris (the Louvre), Stockholm, and London, whose faces and *vermiculé* decoration place them about 1200. On the other hand, the Boston and Oxford pieces probably predate the Baltimore, Amiens, Kansas City, and Cluny examples, where the simplified garments and swayed, attenuated bodies suggest a date about 1230.[15]

The image of Christ on the Cross clothed and crowned as the triumphant ruler has its origin in Revelations (1:13). The dalmatic and alb, unprecedented on crucifixes,[16] should not be mistaken for either the colobium of early medieval representations or the long-sleeved, belted tunics of twelfth-and thirteenth-century wooden crucifixes (especially popular in Catalonia and Roussillon), derived from the famous votive image of the *Volto-Santo* in Lucca.[17]

1. Statens Historiska Museum acc. no. 10603. See Gauthier 1972, pp. 115-116, 340 no. 71; Andersson 1976, pp. 112-117; Andersson 1980, pp. 20-21.

2. Walters Art Gallery acc. no. 44108. See Thoby 1953, pp. 145-146, no. 90.

3. Museu Arqueològic Artistic Episcopal acc. no. 1876. See Thoby 1953, p. 161, no. 3.

4. Victoria and Albert Museum acc. no. 834.1891.

5. Museo de Bellas Artes Cataluna acc. no. 4556. See Ainaud de Lasarte 1973, pp. 212-214.

6. Ashmolean Museum acc. no. 1887.2391. See Caudron 1976, pp. 140-145.

7. Hermitage acc. no. 182. (Formerly Bouvier Collection, before 1884 Basilewsky Collection.) See Lapkovskaya 1971, pp. 16-17; Rupin 1890, p. 256, fig. 319.

8. Bibliothèque Municipale acc. nos. 25 and 26. Both examples are from the collection of Charles de l'Escalopier.

9. Keir Collection. See Stokstad 1983, p. 51, no. 40.

10. Acc. no. OA 8102. (Formerly Martin le Roy collection.) See Marquet de Vasselot 1906, vol. 1, no. 23, pl. 16.

11. Acc. no. Cl 959.

12. Formerly Staatliche Museen, Berlin, acc. no. 1917.98.

13. Eglise de Montlevon. See Rupin 1890, pp. 256-257, fig. 318.

14. Collection of M. de La Villarmois. See Barbier de Montault 1898, p. 575.

15. See Caudron 1976, pp. 140-145.

16. Gauthier 1972, p. 117.

17. On the *Volto Santo* type, see Durliat 1956; Hausherr 1962, pp. 129-170.

24

PLAQUE WITH BISHOP SAINT
Limoges, first quarter of 13th century
Champlevé enamel and gilding on copper
H: 147 mm. (5¹³/₁₆ in.) W: 88 mm. (3⁷/₁₆ in.)
50.2   *Helen and Alice Colburn Fund*

PROVENANCE: Vienna; Leopold Blumka, New York

DESCRIPTION: A mandorla-shaped plaque with six
pinholes. Hammered, *champlevé*, engraved, enameled,
and gilded. The enamel colors are lapis blue, azure
blue, light blue, turquoise, and red in single and mixed
fields of up to three colors. The standing, nimbed
bishop, engraved and in reserve, is placed against an
azure-blue ground decorated in reserve with foliate
scrolls with trefoil and profile leaves. A turquoise band
forms a border. The bearded bishop, who raises his
right arm in benediction, wears a miter, dalmatic, alb,
chasuble, and amice. Over the chasuble is a crosshatched pallium. The dalmatic is decorated with a
rinceaux border on the bottom, and the collar of the
chasuble is marked by an undulating band. The crook
of the crosier in the bishop's left hand takes the form of
one of the foliate ground scrolls. The halo is azure blue
with a light-blue border and red center, and the
pointed ecclesiastical shoes are decorated with central
wavy bands.

CONDITION: There are minute losses of enamel and
some abrasion of the gilding, especially on the
chasuble.

Plaques of this size and shape were applied to
both crosses[1] and reliquary *châsses*.[2] Given that
the present iconography[3] would be unusual on a
cross, the latter use is more likely. The *châsse* in
question may well have held this bishop's relics
and may have been similar to that in the Keir
collection containing the relics of two bishops
from the Limousin, Saints Valerie and Martial,
who are shown standing on the short sides.[4]

The precisely drawn drapery of the present
figure suggests a full body beneath the swinging
curves of the chasuble. The figure style is comparable to that on the enameled plaques of the
early-thirteenth-century Shrine of Saint Dulcide
in Chamberet.[5]

1. See no. 25 and Thoby 1953.
2. See, for example, Rupin 1890, p. 417, fig. 474.
3. The only other plaques of the same subject show
enthroned bishops. They are found on a coffer in the
Treasury of Sant'Eligio dei Fabbri in Rome; in the
Fürstlich Hohenzollernsches Museum in Sigmaringen
(acc. no. 5120); in the Bibliothèque Municipale in
Amiens; and in the Fitzwilliam Museum in Cambridge
(acc. no. 28a-28b-1904; see Dalton 1912, p. 101, nos.
49-50).
4. See Gauthier and François 1981, p. 26, no. 32.
5. See Rupin 1890, pp. 116-119.

25

PLAQUE WITH STANDING CHRIST
Limoges, first third of 13th century
Champlevé enamel on copper
H: 124 mm. (4^{15}/16 in.) W: 90 mm. (3^{9}/16 in.)
85.86   *Gift of Estate of Alfred Greenough*

PROVENANCE: Alfred Greenough, Milton,
Massachusetts

DESCRIPTION: Mandorla-shaped plaque with eight
pinholes. Hammered, *champlevé*, engraved, enameled,
and gilded. Enamel colors are lapis blue, turquoise,
light blue, white, yellow, green, and red in single and
mixed fields of three colors. Christ, engraved and in
reserve, stands full face with open palms on a lapis-blue
ground. His green halo, with red dots and yellow
border, contains a gilded cross. Within an inner turquoise and an outer hatched reserved border, the lapis-
blue ground has reserved crosses and four discs (the
lower two with reserved rosettes and the upper two in
reserve with enameled quatrefoils of red, light blue,
and white). Two hands are engraved on the reverse.

CONDITION: There are considerable losses of enamel,
and the gilding is almost completely abraded.

The plaque probably comes from the central
crossing on the back side of a cross. Such crosses,
with enamels mounted on a wooden core, were
made in large quantity in Limoges workshops
during the twelfth and thirteenth centuries.
Those with mandorla-shaped crossings are
thought to be datable between 1190 and 1235.
Earlier examples tend to be round, and square
crossings do not appear until the second half of
the thirteenth century.[1] The front is usually decorated with a crucified Christ, often crowned and
in relief (see no. 23); surrounding figures include
Mary, John, and Peter. On the back, the triumphant Christ, either seated or standing, is usually
surrounded by symbols of the Evangelists.[2]

As a rule, the triumphant Christ is shown
blessing, but occasionally he appears with open
palms, revealing wounds. (The wounds are missing in the Boston example.) A seated Christ in
this pose is found on the Bonneval Cross in the
Cluny Museum in Paris,[3] and a standing figure,
especially close to Boston's, appears on another
cross in the Cluny.[4] Plaques with similar iconography are in collections in Lillehamen,[5] Budapest,[6] London,[7] Liverpool (formerly),[8] and the
Vatican.[9]

The loosely sketched drapery, falling close to
the body in V-shaped curves, and the wavy cap-
like hair are closely paralleled on the standing
Christs of the Cluny cross and the Vatican plaque
mentioned above. The three are probably contemporary and are in the style of the early thirteenth century.

1. See Gauthier 1978b, p. 274.

2. For Limoges crosses, see Thoby 1953.

3. Acc. no. Cl 2888. See Gauthier 1978b.

4. Acc. no. Cl 985. See Thoby 1953, pp. 108-109, no. 31.

5. Sandvigske Samlinger-Maihaugen. See Mowinckel
1925, pp. 5-23.

6. National Museum acc. no. 34.1894.2. See Kovacs
1968, p. 50, pls. 4-5.

7. Victoria and Albert Museum acc. no. 210.1956.

8. Collection of Phillip Nelson.

9. Museo Sacro Vaticano acc. no. 867. See Stohlman
1939, p. 40, no. 52.

26

EUCHARISTIC DOVE
Limoges, first half of 13th century
Champlevé enamel and gilding on copper
H: 177 mm. (6¹⁵⁄₁₆ in.) W: 220 mm. (8 in.)
D: 85 mm. (3⁵⁄₁₆ in.)
49.1075   *William Francis Warden Fund*

PROVENANCE: Léonce Alexandre Rosenberg, Paris
(sale, Hôtel Drouot, Paris, June 12, 1924, no. 59);
Octave Pincot, Paris (sale, Hôtel Drouot, Paris, November 25, 1946, no. 47); Raphael Stora, New York

BIBLIOGRAPHY: G. Swarzenski 1951, pp. 17-18, fig.
2; *Boston Museum Bulletin* 1957, p. 82. no. 33;
Gauthier 1973, pp. 171-172, fig. 1

EXHIBITIONS: Cambridge 1975, no. 18, pp. 93-94,
ill. p. 127

DESCRIPTION: The dove is constructed of two sides
soldered together and reinforced with rivets (see radiograph, fig. 8). The tail, consisting of an upper enameled plaque and a lower gilded and engraved one, is
soldered and riveted to the body. The enameled and
engraved wings, which cross over the tail, are attached
with rivets. Under the hinged right forewing is an oval
receptacle for the host (H: 50 mm.; W: 66 mm.; D: 49
mm.) constructed from one curved piece of gilded
copper soldered to a base plate. The blue glass eyes are
attached to a rivet; the beak of cast brass is the end of a
rivet extending to the back of the head; and the legs of
solid copper serve as rivets attaching the feet and circular enameled base to the body. Enamel colors are lapis
blue, red, green, yellow, and light blue. Plumage is
simulated by engraving done on the gilt body after the
bird was assembled. The wings and tail are enameled
with linear and scale patterns and inset with turquoise
and dark-blue stones on punched diagonal bands. The
circular lapis-blue base has a central enameled rosette
surrounded by thin *rinceaux* ending alternately in
reserved and enameled trefoil leaves.

CONDITION: Extensive losses of enamel on the wings
and tail have been restored with painted plaster. The
gilding is abraded, particularly on the underside. The
hinge and lockpin are replacements and the solder
repairing a break on the underside of the tail is
modern.

Used for storing consecrated wafers, eucharistic
doves of this type were attached to base plates
and suspended by chains above the altar,[1] signify-
ing the presence of the Holy Spirit at the mass.[2]
Such doves were produced in quantity in
Limoges workshops during the first half of the
thirteenth century. Of the forty-two that have
been recorded, about six may be modern and
twelve are now lost.[3] While those that are extant
conform to the same basic formula, each varies
slightly in size, shape, and decoration; no two
appear to have been made from the same mold.
The present example, one of the most finely
proportioned and executed, is unique in the
placement of its receptacle under the wing rather
than on the back. Also unusual are the crossed
wings; they are found as well on a dove in the
Kestner Museum in Hanover[4] and one formerly
in the von Hirsch Collection in Basel.[5] The
rosette and *rinceaux* designs on the enameled
base, common in Limoges metalwork throughout the first half of the thirteenth century, confirm the date.[6]

1. For examples, see Rupin 1890, pp. 223-234;
Gauthier 1973, pp. 171-190.

2. In Western eucharistic theology the Holy Spirit is
thought to issue from Christ, first at his baptism and
subsequently at each consecration of the host. Thus,
these doves, as symbols of the Holy Spirit, surround
the wafers, i.e., the flesh of Christ from which the
Spirit was believed to have emerged. See Cambridge
1975, pp. 86-90.

3. See Gauthier 1973, pp. 174-176.

4. Acc. no. 481. See Stuttmann 1966, pp. 74-75, no.
73.

5. Sale, Sotheby Parke-Bernet, London, June 22,
1978, no. 239.

6. Gauthier (1973, p. 179) has used the same method
of comparing ornamental motifs to date more precisely
other doves with less common designs on their bases.

27

BOX WITH BUSTS OF ANGELS

Limoges, first half of 13th century (with modern additions)

Champlevé enamel and gilding on copper

H: 25 mm. (1 in.) W: 66 mm. (2⅝ in.) D: 37 mm. (1⁷⁄₁₆ in.)

54.1565   Gift of Leopold Blumka

PROVENANCE: M. Boy, Paris (sale, Georges Petit, May 24, 1905, no. 156); Leopold Blumka, New York

EXHIBITIONS: Cambridge 1975, no. 13, pp. 79-80

DESCRIPTION: Rectangular box with trefoil hinge and broken clasp. Enamels are hammered, bent, soldered, *champlevé*, engraved, enameled, and gilded. The box has a soldered base and interior divider providing two compartments. Sides are a single strip bent at the corners and attached in the middle of the left side. Enamel colors are lapis blue, azure blue, white, red, green, and yellow in single and mixed fields of up to three colors. Reserved and engraved busts of angels with spread wings emerging from clouds (paired on the front and lid and one on each of the short sides) sit against a lapis-blue ground filled with small reserved dots. Angels on the front have green halos with red dots edged in yellow. The other halos are azure blue with red dots and a white border. On the back is a reserved cross pattern on red ground. Reserve bands engraved with an undulating line frame each side. The interior is ungilded.

CONDITION: The lid, clasp (broken), and hinges are replacements made after 1905, when the box appeared in the Boy sale with a plain iron cover. Technical analyses reveal that the compositions of the enamel on the body differ from those of the enamel on the lid. On the body, there are small losses of enamel, and the gilding is almost completely abraded.

The liturgical use of this box, divided into two compartments (each 32 x 35 x 21 mm.) is uncertain. With similar dimensions and an interior partition, a thirteenth-century Limoges enameled box with foliate designs, formerly in the Musée Municipal in Limoges,[1] probably served the same purpose. Both may have held two relics, as is suggested by the only other small box known that was originally divided in the same manner: a twelfth-century English silver reliquary with niello decoration showing scenes from the martyrdom of Saint Thomas à Becket and thought to have held two vials of this saint's blood.[2]

The decoration on the sides of the Boston box (busts of angels) resembles that on larger caskets from Limoges, the "*bôites aux saintes huiles*" used to store the three holy oils.[3] The interior of these caskets contains a horizontal copper plate pierced with three holes to receive vials. Lacking evidence, however, that containers were made for only two of the three oils, it is not possible to draw further parallels between these and the Boston box.

The size of the compartments and the modest dimensions of the box itself prompt speculation that it held two hosts, and thus may have been used by priests to carry Communion to the sick. References to such viatic pyxes are found as early as the ninth and tenth centuries,[4] but their precise design is unknown.

Before it was realized that the lid with its unique figure style was modern, the box was thought to be the work of a North German artist imitating Limoges models.[5] The style of the enamels on the sides of the box, however, present no problems for assigning the piece to a Limoges workshop in the first half of the thirteenth century. The angels may be compared to those on two ciboria, one in the Musée du Louvre in Paris by G. Alpais[6] and the other in the British Museum,[7] and to those on a pyx in the Walters Art Gallery in Baltimore.[8]

1. Acc. no. 54.301. See Limoges 1977, p. 53; and Gauthier 1968, pp. 449-450.

2. Metropolitan Museum, New York, acc. no. 17.190.520. See London 1984, p. 282, no. 302.

3. See Rupin 1890, pp. 443-446. See also a casket formerly in the Rütschi Collection (sale, Galerie Fischer, Lucerne, September 5, 1931, no. 16).

4. See Cambridge 1975, pp. 66, 80.

5. Ibid., p. 80.

6. Acc. no. 67. See Gauthier 1950, frontispiece and pl. 15.

7. Acc. no. 53. 1L18. See British Museum 1924, fig. 47.

8. Acc. no. 44.103.

28

PYX
Limoges, first half of 13th century
Champlevé enamel and gilding on copper
H: 95 mm. (3¼ in.) DIAM.: 69 mm. (2¼ in.)
15.322   *Gift of Horatio G. Curtis*

PROVENANCE: Johann Bossard, Lucerne, 1889;
Horatio G. Curtis, Boston

EXHIBITIONS: "Exhibition of Ecclesiastical Arts,"
Museum of Fine Arts, Springfield, 1941

DESCRIPTION: Round container, enameled and
gilded outside and gilded inside, with a conical lid, a
knob on top, hinge, and clasp. The bottom is attached
by six mortise-and-tenon joints; the seams of the lid
and body are aligned with the hinge. The copper
plaques are bent and soldered, *champlevé*, engraved,
enameled, and gilded. Enamel colors are lapis blue,
turquoise, and white in single fields. Against a lapis-
blue ground, white medallions with the monogram of
Christ (three on the lid and four on the bottom)
alternate with heart-shaped tendrils surrounding five-
petaled palmettes in reserve on a turquoise ground.
The monogram IHS with an abbreviation mark above
and gilded cross below is in its proper form in the
upper medallions but is inverted SHI on the body.
Gilded bands with double rows of engraved dots frame
the enamel fields.

CONDITION: The cross on top and the lockpin are
missing. The gilding is abraded and there are small
losses of enamel on the body.

The word pyx derives from a transliteration of
the Greek πύξις meaning boxwood receptacle.
Used to store the consecrated host, tower-shaped
pyxes like the present one were made in large
quantity in Limoges workshops during the thirteenth century. Although nearly uniform in size
and shape, and decorated with a limited reper-
toire of ornamental patterns, figural subjects, and
monograms, no two containers are identical. On
the present example, both the IHS monogram on
a white disc (an allusion to the contents of the
container) and the palmettes with five petals
(whose shape echoes that of the container) are
common forms.[1] Closely related are a pyx formerly in the Rütschi Collection [2] and one in the
Wadsworth Athenaeum in Hartford;[3] the latter,
like the present example, combines both the cor-
rect and inverted forms of the monogram.

Given the repetition of decorative motifs in the
Limoges workshop throughout the first half of
the thirteenth century, precise dating of these
objects is difficult to establish.

1. On pyxes, see Rupin 1890, pp. 201-222; Bilimoff
1978.
2. Alfred Rütschi, Zurich (sale, Galerie Fischer,
Lucerne, September 5, 1931, no. 9).
3. Acc. no. 1966.527. See Hartford 1967, p. 30, fig. 1.

29

PYX
Limoges, first half of 13th century
Champlevé enamel and gilding on copper
H: 86 mm. (3⅜ in.) DIAM.: 68 mm. (2¹¹⁄₁₆ in.)
61.209 *Gift of Dr. Charles J. White*

PROVENANCE: T. F. Richardson, Washington, D.C.

DESCRIPTION: Round container, enameled outside
and gilded inside, with a conical lid, knob on top,
hinge, and clasp. The bottom plaque is attached by six
mortise-and-tenon joints. Copper plaques are bent and
soldered, *champlevé*, engraved, enameled, and gilded.
Enamel colors are lapis blue and white in single fields.
On both the body and the lid, gilded bands with two
rows of engraved dots frame lapis-blue grounds containing reserved discs (six on the body, four on the
lid). Separated by engraved and gilded curved stems
with profile leaves, the discs (engraved only on the lid)

contain white asters with eight petals and gilded
centers.

CONDITION: The lockpin and the cross on top are
missing. The gilding is considerably abraded, and there
are small losses of enamel.

Notable on this pyx is the balancing of the design
on the top with that on the body. White asters
with either six or eight petals are common on
Limoges pyxes, but they are usually placed
against turquoise discs.[1] The simple curved tendrils separating the medallions are also found on
a pyx in the Cluny Museum in Paris.[2]

1. See Bilimoff 1978, p. 50; Rupin 1890, p. 207, fig.
268.
2. Acc. no. 14790. See Limoges 1948, no. 116.

30

ROUNDEL WITH BASILISKS
Limoges, first half of 13th century
Champlevé enamel and gilding on copper
DIAM.: 93 mm. (3¹¹⁄₁₆ in.)
47.1038   *H. E. Bolles Fund*

PROVENANCE: Adolph Loewi, Los Angeles

DESCRIPTION: Round plaque with enameled border, gilded openwork center, and four attachment holes. Hammered, *champlevé*, engraved, *repoussé*, cut out, enameled, and gilded. Enamel colors are lapis blue, turquoise, white, and red. Two basilisks chased with scales, one on top of the other, bite each other's necks. On the border white enamel bands outline overlapping arches whose grounds are filled alternately with lapis-blue and turquoise enamel. The smaller turquoise arches contain two engraved gilded leaves, while the larger lapis-blue arches surround engraved gilded palmettes with red enamel between the leaves.

CONDITION: The stippled outer border has lost most of its gilding, and the lapis-blue enamel ground next to the border appears to be modern. Gilding is worn in several places, and there are small losses of enamel, especially around attachment holes.

Made to decorate wooden caskets, this and similar examples display various related enamel designs and intertwined beasts in openwork.[1] This roundel comes from the same series as two of identical dimensions and with similar central designs and frames. One is in the Musée des Beaux Arts in Lyon;[2] the other is in the Müseum für Kunsthandwerk in Frankfurt.[3] The three are closely related in size and decoration to those on a casket in a private collection in Italy.[4]

1. For example, see Rupin 1890, pp. 436-442; Mallé 1950, pp. 80-122; Verlet 1950, pp. 6-7; Gauthier 1972, p. 376, no. 139; Gauthier and François 1981, p. 25, nos. 29-30; Cologne 1985, vol. I, pp. 340-343, nos. B117-119, B121.

2. Acc. no. D77.

3. Acc. no VI82/769. See Frankfurt 1982, no. 8, pl. I.

4. Formerly Cardinal Guala Bichieri Collection. See Mallé 1950, pp. 80-88.

31

RELIEF OF CHRIST ENTHRONED
Limoges, second quarter of 13th century
Champlevé enamel and gilding on copper
H: 83 mm. (3¼ in.) W: 42 mm. (1⅝ in.) D: 13
mm. (9/16 in.)
49.1203 *Arthur Mason Knapp Fund*

PROVENANCE: French and Company, New York

DESCRIPTION: Seated figure in low relief; two
pinholes. Single copper sheet, cut out, *repoussé, champlevé*, chased, engraved, enameled, and gilded. Enamel
colors are white, yellow, and lapis blue in single fields.
The crown with a central protruding cross and blue
enamel band is attached; the eyes are inlaid with light-
blue stones. Draped in a tunic with a yellow collar and
a pallium with engraved folds, the seated Christ lifts his
right arm in benediction and raises a closed white
book, close to his side, in his left hand. His hair falls
close to the head. The feet rest on a crosshatched
crescent.

CONDITION: The gilding is abraded, especially in
areas of high relief. The left eye is missing, and the
central attachment hole has been enlarged.

This enthroned Christ belongs to a well-docu-
mented group of reliefs found on Limoges crosiers of the thirteenth century. Larger examples
of the same type of seated Christ are applied to
processional crosses and reliquaries from
Limoges.[1] Within the volutes of the crosiers, on
oval or polylobed engraved plaques, each relief is
mounted back-to-back with a similar one showing a seated Virgin and Child. The reliefs applied
to twenty-five crosiers of this type assembled by
J.J. Marquet de Vasselot[2] vary in style and quality
of execution. On some the drapery is completely
enameled; others have no enamel at all.

The simple engraved folds of the present piece
suggest a style derived from the soft classicizing
draperies with raised folds on larger Limoges
reliefs like those on two tabernacles, one in the
Cathedral Treasury at Chartres and the other in
the Metropolitan Museum in New York, datable
about 1225-1235.[3] The most splendid examples
of this style are the six large Apostles thought to
come from the destroyed altar frontal of the
abbey at Grandmont.[4] For the present relief,
then, a slightly later date seems most likely.

1. For examples, see Gauthier 1972, p. 373, nos. 132-
133; Thoby 1953, p. 109, no. 32.

2. Marquet de Vasselot 1941, pp. 67-74, 212-229, pls.
9-10. On Limoges crosiers, see also Rupin 1890, pp.
551-564.

3. Acc. no. 17.190.735 (New York). See Gauthier
1972, pp. 184-187, and 372-373, nos. 130-131;
Gauthier 1978a, pp. 23-42.

4. See Souchal 1963, pp. 126-130.

32

RELIEF OF BAPTISM OF CHRIST
Limoges, mid-13th century
Champlevé enamel and gilding on copper
H: 368 mm. (14⁹⁄16 in.) W: 211 mm. (8¼ in.)
D: 28 mm. (1¹⁄16 in.)
50.858 *Francis Bartlett Fund*

PROVENANCE: Louis Germeau, Paris (sale, Hôtel Drouot, Paris, May 5, 1868, no. 51); Countess Dzialynska, Paris; Prince Wladyslaw Czartoryski, Goluchow Castle, Poznan, Poland; J. Pollack, Paris; Wildenstein and Company, New York

BIBLIOGRAPHY: Darcel 1865, pp. 439-440; Giraud 1881, pl. 3; Garnier 1886, pp. 426-427; Rupin 1890, pp. 358-359, fig. 423; Molinier 1903, p. 39, pl. 6; G. Swarzenski 1951, pp. 17-25, fig. 1; *Boston Museum Bulletin* 1957, pp. 80-81, no. 32; Hunter 1958, p. 29; Rückert 1959, p. 7; Le Goff 1964, p. 432, fig. 162; H. Swarzenski 1969, p. 488, no. 9; Otavsky 1973, p. 59, fig. 14; Gauthier 1978a, p. 35; Boston 1981, no. 37; Steinberg 1983, pp. 136-137, fig. 154

EXHIBITIONS: "Exposition de l'Union Centrale des Beaux-Arts appliqués à l'industrie," Paris, 1865, no. 617; "Exposition de l'Union Centrale des Beaux-Arts appliqués à l'industrie," Paris, 1880. no. 2; Cleveland 1967, pp. 130-133, no. IV 4

DESCRIPTION: Relief with three pinholes (in the ewer and lower corners) representing John the Baptist in three-quarter view pouring water from a ewer over a nimbed frontal Christ. With his right arm raised in benediction, Christ stands immersed to the thighs in water (the river Jordan). Single copper sheet, *repoussé* (into a mold), cut out, *champlevé*, engraved, chased, enameled, and gilded. The blue glass eyes are inset. Both figures have finely chased long hair and beards. Curved segments of white enamel indicate the movement of the water, in which fish are in reserve and engraved. All except two swim to the left. Saint John's garment is chased to indicate fur on the outside.

CONDITION: Small areas where enamel has been lost (especially near the edges) are filled with plaster paste. The gilding is completely abraded in spots. Cracks in the metal occur between the rim of the ewer and the water, and between Christ and the water bordering his left side. An original break in the lower left corner has been repaired by soldering an additional piece of copper onto the back.[1] The lower pinholes, which do not appear in early reproductions and whose edges betray a modern drill, are not original.

Distinct from most Limoges metalwork, which with minor variations follows standard formulas, this Baptism is a unique creation of exceptional quality. It was probably mounted on an enameled ground with vegetal designs and was one of a series of similar reliefs depicting scenes from the Life of Christ on a retable or an altar frontal. Like those destroyed at the end of the eighteenth century at Bourganeuf, the Collégiale of Saint Martial de Limoges, and Grandmont, such ensembles are known only from descriptions.[2]

Two common features in representations of the Baptism – the dove symbolizing the Holy Spirit and the angel holding Christ's garment – are missing here. Either or both may have been included in the original design as separate reliefs. The scene is unusual also in representing baptism both *per infusionem* and *per immersionem* – probably a combination of local iconographic traditions. The first – with John the Baptist pouring from a ewer and Christ raising his right hand in a gesture of blessing – is depicted in a Limoges Gospel Book from the mid-twelfth century;[3] the second – with a frontal Christ immersed in rippling water with fish – is shown in a Limoges manuscript of the early thirteenth century in New York.[4]

Although not enameled like the Baptism, seven scenes from Christ's Infancy and Passion of comparable size and style probably belong to the same ensemble.[5] Closest to the Boston relief, and possibly by the same master, are a Flagellation in the Musée Cluny in Paris,[6] an Entombment in the Minneapolis Institute of Arts,[7] a Crucifixion composed of reliefs in various collections,[8] and a Deposition in the Abegg Collection in Riggisberg.[9] Reliefs from the same series that are clearly by different hands are a Betrayal[10] in the Walters Art Gallery in Baltimore, a Last Supper in the Musée Cluny,[11] and Three Magi from an Adoration, now divided among several collections.[12] All have similar elongated figures with drapery marked by deep teardrop-shaped depressions, suggesting a date about 1240-1250. In style and execution they are most closely related to the large Limoges head reliquaries and to two tombs in the Cathedral of Saint Denis.[13]

1. This type of repair occurs on several of the related reliefs mentioned below. See Gauthier 1967, p. 119; Otavsky 1973, pp. 38-40, 65.

2. See Cleveland 1967, p. 133. For Bourganeuf, see the description of October 1772 in Rupin 1890, pp. 100, 197. For Grandmont, see Gaborit 1976, pp. 231-246, with additional bibliography. Similar reliefs of smaller scale are mounted on enameled ground on the tabernacles from the Cathedral Treasury at Chartres and that from Cherves-en-Angoumois, now in the Metropolitan Museum in New York (acc. no. 17.190.735; see Gauthier 1978a, pp. 23-42).

3. Bibliothèque Nationale, Paris, lat. 252. See Gaborit-Chopin 1969, p. 179, fig. 180.

4. Morgan Library M.44. See G. Swarzenski 1951, pp. 21-22, fig. 4.

5. The group of reliefs was put together initially by G. Swarzenski (1951, pp. 17-25). Five were assembled in the exhibition "Treasures from Medieval France" at the Cleveland Museum in 1967. In the nineteenth century several were together in the Germeau collection. See Otavsky 1973, p. 58 n. 35.

6. Acc. no. 942. See Cleveland 1967, pp. 130-133, no. IV 7.

7. Acc. no. 58.8. (Formerly in the Collection of Kenneth Clark, London, and with the present relief in the Collection of Prince Wladyslaw Czartoryski.) See Hunter 1958, pp. 26-32.

8. Two Maries in the Abegg-Stiftung in Riggisberg (acc. no. 8.59.63), a crucifix in the Musée de Picardie in Amiens, and a centurion in the Musée du Louvre in Paris (acc. no. OA 10625, formerly Nicholas Landau, Paris). A figure of John, now lost but formerly reused on a nineteenth-century shrine (see no. 16) with the Maries and the centurion, may also have been part of the Crucifixion scene. See Otavsky 1973, pp. 37-74.

9. Acc. no. 8.191.72. (Formerly in the Salavin Collection in Paris.) See Otavsky 1973, pp. 42-74.

10. Acc. no. 53.10. See Cleveland 1967, pp. 130-133, no. IV 6.

11. Acc. no. 973. See ibid., no. IV 5.

12. Kestner Museum in Hanover, acc. no. 474; C. Ratton, Paris; and a private collection in Brussels. The authors are grateful to Karel Otavsky for bringing these to their attention.

Three related reliefs are somewhat different in style and probably later in date: the miracle scene in the Musée Jacquemart André in Chaalis (acc. no. 71; see Otavsky 1973, pp. 60-62; Gaborit 1976, pp. 241-242); the group of Apostles (probably from an Ascension) in the collection of Martin Le Roy (see Marquet de Vasselot 1906, no. 37); and a single figure in the Musée des Beaux-Arts in Poitiers (acc. no. 947-21-1265; see Sandoz 1959, no. 44).

13. Those of Jean de France (d. 1248) and his sister Blanchis. See Rückert 1959, pp. 4-8; Otavsky 1973, pp. 58-74; Gauthier 1978a, p. 35.

enlarged detail

33

CIRCULAR HINGED CASE
Limoges or Limoges workshop in Paris, third
quarter of 13th century
Champlevé enamel and gilding on copper
DIAM.: 62 mm. (2⁷/₁₆ in.) D: 17 mm. (¹¹/₁₆ in.)
49.470 *William Francis Warden Fund*

PROVENANCE: Lord Carmichael of Skirling, London
(sale, Sotheby's, June 10, 1926, no. 10); George
Eumorphopoulos, London (sale, Sotheby's, June 6,
1940, no. 186); Joseph Brummer, New York (sale,
Parke-Bernet, April 23, 1949, no. 696)

BIBLIOGRAPHY: G. Swarzenski 1949, pp. 79-80, fig.
7; *Boston Museum Bulletin* 1957, p. 77, no. 25

EXHIBITIONS: Birmingham 1936, no. 63; London
1936, no. 95; Ottawa 1972, pp. 138-139, no. 54, pl.
76; Ann Arbor 1975, no. 86, pp. 119-120, pl. 8

DESCRIPTION: Round container comprising two
similar valves (each with small retaining pins on the
sides) fastened with a hinge and clasp. Hammered,
champlevé, engraved, chased, enameled, and gilded.
Enamel colors are lapis blue, red, and turquoise. On
the cover, within a narrow turquoise border, a red
armorial shield with three trefoils of acanthus in
reserve is set against a dark-blue ground with three
wingless dragons, also in reserve. On the opposite side,
again encircled by a turquoise border, an amorous
couple is engraved in reserve against a lapis-blue
ground with thin foliate scrolls in reserve. The female,
in three-quarter view on the left, stands taller than her
mate on a gilded platform in the border. She wears a
snood with a lozenge design and a long mantle over a
dress with a gathered waist and decorated collar.
Caressing her under the chin, her lover, in profile on
the right, is clad in a short tunic and pointed shoes.
The sides of each valve are decorated with a row of
curved trefoil leaves.

CONDITION: There are significant losses of enamel.
Repairs on the turquoise borders have been made with
red wax, and painted paste has been used to fill gaps in
the blue ground. Gilding is considerably abraded.

The courtly subject and coat of arms indicate that
this is an object for personal use.[1] Several comparisons, as well as the small retaining pins on the
sides (possibly used to secure inserts) suggest
that it is a mirror case.[2] (As such, it should be
seen as a precursor of the popular ivory mirror
backs of the fourteenth century with similar
scenes of lovers.[3]) The hinged design of the present box is similar to that on an earlier and

smaller mirror case with a long handle in the
Museum für Kunsthandwerk in Frankfurt.[4] A
mirror box in the Louvre,[5] of contemporary
Limoges manufacture and decorated with arms,
is closest in execution to the present example,
although it is somewhat larger and has no hinge.
Finally, there is another comparable French mirror case in The Cloisters in New York[6] (now
missing its back) whose front, showing the arms
of Lusignan of Poitou, has holes for retaining
pins similar to those on the present piece.

Although the Boston box is clearly executed in
the manner of Limoges work, its drapery style
appears to be unique among contemporary
enamels. It cannot, as previously assumed, have
been executed by the same Limoges artist who
made an unusual cylindrical box in Paris[7] showing four pairs of lovers; on close inspection, the
finely detailed, flowing drapery ending in undulating folds on the Paris box is unlike Boston's.
On the latter, the elongated, lithe figures with
thin drapery forming complex angles are closest
to those in the Psalter of Saint Louis,[8] a manuscript made in Paris about 1253-1270. Thus, a
similar date should be assigned to the Boston
case.[9] If, as has been suggested, there were
Limoges workshops in Paris[10] this would be
likely to have been produced in one of them.

1. Philippe Verdier (Ottawa 1972, p. 139, no. 54) and
Meredith Lillich ("Gothic Heraldry and Name Pun-
ning: Secular Iconography on a Box of Limoges
Enamel," *Journal of Medieval History*, forthcoming)
have proposed that the box served as a case for a
hinged seal matrix, but such a case would be the only
example of its kind. Furthermore, the matrix, with its
protruding hinge, would not have fitted snugly in the
round container.
    Meredith Lillich has suggested that the heraldic arms
are those of Jean II de Prie, Lord of Buzançais (Berry)
from 1275 to 1317. She interprets the courtly scene on
the other side as a rebus representing the French verb
prier, a pun on the family name, meaning to beseech or
to beg of (see Lillich, above). The Prie arms are indeed
gueules à trois tiercefeuilles d'or (see Brault 1973, p. 28),
but it is not certain that the present trefoils are
tiercefeuilles, which normally have a different smooth-
edged form. The authors are grateful to D'A. J. Boulton for his assistance on heraldry.

2. See G. Swarzenski 1949, pp. 79-80.

3. See, for example, Koechlin 1924, pp. 366-367, nos. 988, 993.

4. Acc. no. 6744. The bronze case showing a loving couple in relief is thought to be Swabian and datable to the mid-twelfth century. See Stuttgart 1977, p. 219, no. 269.

5. Acc. no. OA 6281. (Formerly Victor Gay Collection.) See Rupin 1890, pp. 576-577. Here one side is cut to fit into the other.

6. Acc. no. 50.7.4. See Ostoia 1959, pp. 18-27. The arms indicate the case was produced about 1300. It has holes on the sides for small retaining pins identical to those on the Boston case.

7. Cluny Museum LOA. 6279. See Gay 1887, p. 168; G. Swarzenski 1949, p. 80.

8. Bibliothèque Nationale, Paris, lat. 10525. See Branner 1977, pp. 132-137 and 238.

9. The snood covering the woman's hair, previously used to date the box to the early fourteenth century (see Ottawa 1972, p. 139, no. 54), does indeed appear in mid-thirteenth-century Parisian manuscripts. (See Branner 1977, figs. 193, 393.)

10. Marie-Madeleine Gauthier (oral communication).

34

FOUR HERALDIC ROUNDELS
Limoges, third quarter of 13th century
Champlevé enamel and gilding on copper
DIAM.: 40 mm. (1⁹⁄₁₆ in.)
57.595-598   *John H. and Ernestine A. Payne Fund*

PROVENANCE: Johannes Jantzen, Bremen

BIBLIOGRAPHY: Chicago 1970, nos. 6, 7, 8, 9

EXHIBITIONS: Providence 1977, no. 25, p. 78

DESCRIPTION: Four openwork *repoussé* roundels with four pinholes. Triangular enameled, heraldic shields are attached with three pins. Roundels: *repoussé*, engraved, chased, and cut out. Shields: *champlevé*, enameled, and gilded. Enamel colors are red and black in single fields. The basilisks in openwork with twisted heads biting their necks and long flowering tails surround a central gilded shield showing a red rampant lion with black claws, tongue, and eye.

CONDITION: The edges are bent and abraded.

With others in Frankfurt,[1] Kassel,[2] and New York,[3] these roundels belong to a group of eleven bearing the same arms. The series was probably mounted originally on a casket. They resemble those of somewhat larger size mounted on the so-called casket of Richard of Cornwallis in Aachen,[4] and the four enameled strips attached to the sides of the Kassel roundel are similar to those found on the same casket. It has recently been suggested that the Aachen piece was made in 1258 in Limoges for the marriage of Marguerite, daughter of Hughes IV de Bourgogne, to Guy VI le Preux, Viscount of Limoges, whose arms are shown in the roundels.[5] Thus, a related date and localization may be proposed for the present series.

Precise identification of the heraldic arms is impossible without additional evidence of provenance, as they were used by at least a dozen noble families, including the Hapsburgs in Austria, the Foucaulds and Du Puys in France, and the Counts of Holland, Unruh, Reckheim, Roucy, and Fife.[6]

1. Museum für Kunsthandwerk acc. no. 12648a-b. See Frankfurt 1966, no. 256, pl. 8.

2. Staatliche Kunstsammlungen acc. no. K5.2401. See Hamburg 1961, no. 287.

3. Collections of Max Falk and Edward R. Lubin. (Formerly Thomas Flannery, Chicago [sale, Sotheby Parke-Bernet, December 1, 1983, no. 35].)

4. See de Vaivre 1974, pp. 97-124.

5. Ibid., pp. 108-120.

6. See Woodward and Burnett 1892, p. 212. Earlier identifications (Frankfurt 1966, no. 256) of these with the Kings of León cannot be substantiated for these should show purple lions on a white (or silver) ground. The authors are grateful to D'A. J. Boulton for this information.

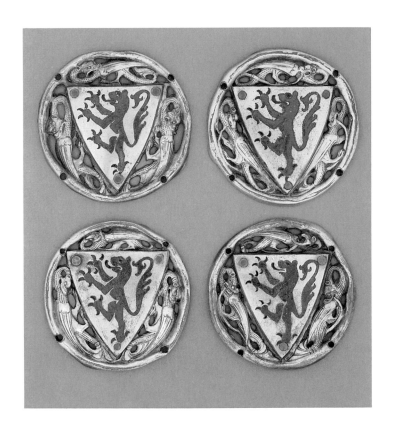

35

ROUND CONTAINER WITH COUPLE
FEASTING
Limoges, second half of 13th century
Champlevé enamel on copper
DIAM: 41 mm. (1⅝ in.) D: 15 mm. (9/16 in.)
55.498 *Anonymous Gift*

PROVENANCE: Alfred Spero, London

BIBLIOGRAPHY: Gauthier and François 1981, p. 25

DESCRIPTION: Lenticular container. Hammered,
champlevé, engraved, chased, enameled, and gilded. A
convex enameled plaque with two uncentered loops for
suspension is soldered to a flat plaque with a rectangular notch at the top for a lid. The ground is lapis blue
with engraved figures in reserve. Seated behind a table
set with (from left to right) a bowl, a beaker, a round
loaf of bread, and a platter of fish are two figures, one
pouring from a jug into a beaker held by the other. A
large quatrefoil fills the ground between their heads.
The reserved border around the scene is decorated
with a double row of chased dots.

CONDITION: The sliding lid is missing, and only
traces remain of gilding on the front. The engraving is
rubbed and large areas of enamel are lost.

Five other containers of this unusual size and
shape are known, all apparently of Limoges
workmanship. The example in the British
Museum,[1] slightly larger than the others, shows a
siren against a *rinceaux* ground. Those in the
Cluny Museum in Paris,[2] the Massena Museum
in Nice,[3] and two in Schloss Köpenick in East
Berlin[4] are decorated with coats of arms and thus
seem to have been commissioned. The domestic
scene on the Boston piece, unique within
Limoges metalwork, suggests that this could be
one of the small containers for precious spices
mentioned in medieval inventories.[5]

Unfortunately, the figures are too rubbed to
permit precise comparisons of style. Their tight-
fitting drapery and loosely sketched faces, comparable to those on a *gemellion* in the Cluny
Museum[6] and a plaque formerly in Limoges,[7]
support a date in the second half of the thirteenth
century.

1. Acc. no. MLA 94.2-17.8.
2. Acc. no. Cl 17.706. See Gay 1887, p. 31. The piece
has a long neck, giving it the shape of a pilgrim flask.
3. Acc. no. 331. The authors are grateful to Geneviève
François for bringing this piece to our attention. See
Apollo 1925, p. 131, pl. 8, where it is mistakenly called
a plaque.
4. Said to have been found in a recent excavation.
5. See Gay 1887, p. 170.
6. Acc. no. 4533. See Gauthier 1950, p. 159, pl. 55.
7. Acc. no. 271 (stolen in 1981 from the Musée
Municipal). See ibid., p. 158, pl. 51.

36

PAIR OF PLAQUES WITH BEASTS
Limoges or Limoges workshop in England, ca. 1300
Champlevé enamel on copper
H: 154 mm. (6¹⁄₁₆ in.) W: 102 mm. (4 in.)
48.1320-1321 *William E. Nickerson Fund*

PROVENANCE: Baron Max von Goldschmidt-Rothschild, Frankfurt; Rosenberg and Stiebel, New York

BIBLIOGRAPHY: G. Swarzenski 1949, pp. 80-81, figs. 8, 9; *Boston Museum Bulletin* 1957, p. 79, no. 31; Gauthier 1972, p. 377

EXHIBITIONS: Ottawa 1972, pp. 137-138, no. 52

DESCRIPTION: Each of the two rectangular plaques has ten pinholes filled with nail heads. Hammered, *champlevé*, chased, engraved, enameled, and gilded. Enamel colors are lapis blue, red, green, azure blue, and white in single and mixed fields of up to three colors. The plaques form a continuous design. Each shows winged beasts in two vertical rows of quatrefoils, which alternate, both vertically and horizontally, between lapis blue and red. Each quatrefoil contains an engraved beast in reserve. They are arranged in either facing or addorsed pairs. The gilded ground, engraved and punched in a stippled pattern, has enameled plants with trefoil leaves (green, blue, and white) alternating with green parrots flanking smaller plants (blue and red).

CONDITION: There are losses of enamel on the upper half of the lower plaque. The gilding is abraded, and the nail heads are modern.

In the early nineteenth century a nearly identical plaque was in the Mansart collection in Beauvais.[1] As part of a series, these three plaques were probably used as sheathing, either on a tomb or on a large *châsse*.[2]

The beasts are typical of Limoges, as are the plants flanked by parrots. This latter motif, which derives from Sicilian silks of the twelfth and thirteenth centuries,[3] is found on openwork medallions on the Limoges casket of Saint Louis in the Louvre (1234-1239)[4] and enamel plaques on the Limoges head of Saint Ferréol in Nexon.[5]

The Boston plaques are most closely related to two arch-shaped plaques with gilded *repoussé* figures, probably from the side of a tomb, in the Wallace Collection in London.[6] Comparable also are the enamel plaques comprising the Valence Casket[7] in the Victoria and Albert Museum in London, a Limoges work clearly made for an English patron. All are made of unusually thick copper and have a similar simplified palette. If, as has been thought, the Valence Casket was commissioned from a Limoges workshop in England, the Boston and Wallace Collection plaques could have a similar origin.[8]

1. Known from an engraving in Willemin (1839, p. 65, pl. 108), where it is said to have been cut into two pieces and reused on a book cover.
2. See, for example, the tomb of William of Valence (d. 1296) in Westminster Abbey (Gauthier 1972, pp. 376-377, no. 141), which has an enameled cushion with a repeating design. For others, see Rupin 1890, pp. 158-164.
3. See Ottawa 1972, pp. 137-138, no. 52.
4. Musée du Louvre acc. no. D940 See de Vaivre 1974, pp. 101-110.
5. Dated by inscription to 1346. See Rupin 1890, pp. 175-177; Paris 1981a, pp. 240-241, no. 194.
6. Acc. nos. 273, 277. See Gauthier 1972, p. 377, no. 142.
7. Acc. no. 4-1895. See ibid., pp. 377-378, no. 143.
8. On the possibility of Limoges workshops having been in England in the thirteenth century, see ibid., pp. 192-195.

MORSE WITH CRUCIFIXION
France, Limoges(?), early 14th century
Champlevé enamel and gilding on copper
H: 173 mm. (6¹³⁄₁₆ in.) W: 176 mm. (6¹⁵⁄₁₆ in.)
49.491 *William Francis Warden Fund*

PROVENANCE: Germeau, Paris (sale, Hôtel Drouot, May 5, 1868, no. 62); Armand Queyroi, Paris (sale, Hôtel Drouot, February 26, 1907, no. 29); Léonce Alexandre Rosenberg, Paris (sale, Hôtel Drouot, June 12, 1924, no. 58); Henri Daguerre, Paris; Joseph Brummer, New York (sale, Parke-Bernet, May 14, 1949, no. 724)

DESCRIPTION: Octafoil plaque with a molded edge representing the Crucifixion in *repoussé*. Hammered into a mold, *champlevé*, engraved, enameled, and gilded. Eleven pinholes are pierced around the edge to sew it to the garment. Larger pinholes at the top and bottom of the cross and four loops soldered to the back are modern. Enamel colors are lapis blue and red. The central Crucifix shows a dead Christ with a cruciform nimbus, long hair and short beard, his head turned to the left. The torso is marked by a series of short parallel lines defining the ribcage, and the loincloth has deep angular folds. The body, twisted to the left, is attached by three nails to the *crux florida*. IH[ESU]s is inscribed on a diagonal panel fastened to the cross. Facing angels holding images of the sun (left) and moon (right) kneel on one knee on the arms of the cross. On the left, the mourning Virgin stands in a swayed posture in three-quarter view with her hands clasped over her breast. Her mantle falls in two large folds down the front. John stands weeping on the right. His lower body is frontal with his feet perched on a corner of the frame, while his torso is turned to the right. In an awkward pose, he raises his draped right hand and holds a book close to his body with his left hand. The two figures have halos decorated with lapis-blue arches against a red ground. The background is lapis blue with six-pointed stars in reserve.

CONDITION: There are considerable losses of enamel from the background, and the gilding is modern.

Used to fasten the cope over the breast, morses of this type belong to a distinct group of the fourteenth century usually assigned to Limoges.[1] All have blue grounds with stars and figures either applied or in *repoussé*. Closest in style to the present example is one in Lyon[2] also representing the Crucifixion. Originally in three parts, its central plaque with the Crucifix is now missing. The figures have the same expressive faces with pointed chins and wide noses, and the Virgin in both cases stands in a similar swayed pose. Other morses of the same type are preserved in Dijon,[3] Paris,[4] Lille,[5] and Toledo, Ohio.[6]

1. See Rupin 1890, pp. 565-566.

2. In the Treasury of the Church of Saint Jean.

3. Musée des Beaux Arts, Collection Trimolet acc. no. 1260, with applied figures representing the Annunciation.

4. Musée du Louvre acc. no. MR.R 251, showing the Virgin and Child flanked by Angels in *repoussé*. See Rupin 1890, fig. 636.

5. Musée des Beaux Arts acc. no. 51, showing the Annunciation in *repoussé*.

6. Toledo Museum of Art acc. no. 50.248, with applied figures representing the Virgin and Child with Christ, Saint Peter, a donor, and an angel.

RELIQUARY TRIPTYCH WITH THE CRUCI-
FIXION, CORONATION OF THE VIRGIN,
SAINT PETER AND SAINT PAUL, AND THE
ANNUNCIATION
Paris or England, early 14th century
Basse-taille and *champlevé* enamel and gilding on
silver
H: 69 mm. (2¹¹⁄₁₆ in.) W (closed): 32 mm. (1¼
in.) W (open): 62 mm. (2⁷⁄₁₆ in.)
58.354 *Theodora Wilbour Fund in Memory of
Charlotte Beebe Wilbour*

PROVENANCE: Baron Max von Goldschmidt-Rothschild, Frankfurt; Rosenberg and Stiebel, New York

BIBLIOGRAPHY: Evans 1953, p. 65; Cleveland 1967,
p. 192; Paris 1981a, pp. 246-247

EXHIBITIONS: Ottawa 1972, pp. 145-146, no. 61,
pls. VI and 83a-b; Providence 1977, no. 27, pp. 80-81

DESCRIPTION: Triptych comprising a central gabled
box with crocketed crest, central finial, and two hinged
wings. When closed, the wings (enameled on both
sides) are held together with a clasp. The sides of the
box, made of a single strip, bent and joined at the top,
have two rows of small crosses separated by a silver
band. Enamel colors are translucent green, mauve,
amber, lapis blue, light turquoise, and opaque red. The
amber glass is placed over gold foil. The Crucifixion on
the inside of the box is composed of cast silver figures
(a Crucified Christ, the Virgin, and Saint John) riveted
to a blue *champlevé* enameled ground, with a lozenge-
and-rosette design in reserve and halos for the figures
in red enamel. The Crucifixion is framed by horizontal
strips of silver, the lower of which forms a receptacle
for a relic. There is a hinge for a cover. When open, the
wings show Saints Peter (right) and Paul (left) with
their backs to the Crucifixion, framed by applied
cusped, trefoil arches. The closed wings show the
Annunciation with Gabriel (on the left shutter) holding a banderole and standing beside a vase of flowers
and the Virgin (on the right shutter) holding a book.
Both figures are placed under trefoil arches above
which are red spandrels with small Vs in reserve, a
band of green enamel with a row of reserved dots
arranged in squares, and sprays of green foliage. The
back represents the Coronation of the Virgin with
Christ (holding an orb with a cross) and the Virgin
seated on a backless throne. Christ blesses his mother
while an angel, emerging from a cloud below the right
trefoil, crowns the Virgin. The dotted diaper grounds
are lapis blue. The heads, hands, and attributes are left
in reserve with the details engraved and filled with
lapis-blue enamel. The figures wear either mauve
tunics with green mantles or green tunics with mauve
mantles. All the mantles are lined with amber. Peter
and Paul have green halos; others are red.

CONDITION: The relic and the lid for its receptacle
are missing. The gilded silver Virgin to the left of the
Crucifix is a replacement. The glass is badly crizzled
and chipped and has been repaired in several places
with wax. Only traces of the gilding remain.

Derived in form from the Byzantine *staurotheca*,
this devotional triptych probably contained a
relic of the True Cross and was kept in the
private chapel of its patron. During the fourteenth century, similar *basse-taille* enamels were
made in France, England, and the Rhineland.
The mobility of craftsmen and the portable
nature of these objects facilitated the transfer of
styles, making precise localization difficult.[1] The
present figure style, characterized by attenuated
bodies, a swayed posture, simply falling drapery
with angular, volumetric curves, and small,
sketchily rendered heads, originated in Paris with
Master Honoré in the last decades of the thirteenth century.[2] The style is found in England as
well in manuscripts like the Queen Mary Psalter,
whose figures provide the closest parallels for
those on the Boston triptych.[3]

   The iconography, however, suggests French
rather than English origin for the present piece.
The angel bringing the crown in the representation of the Coronation (back side) first appears
in the early thirteenth century on the tympanum
of the left portal at Notre Dame in Paris and was
especially common in France.[4] Support for a specifically Parisian origin is provided by the
reserved V motif in the spandrels and the rosette
with five reserved petals and an opaque red
center; both are found in several Parisian
enamels.[5] Furthermore, the trefoil arches above
Peter and Paul, with an almost closed center, are
matched on the stem of a Parisian chalice in
Copenhagen[6] and two small diptychs[7] and a folding altarpiece,[8] also usually assigned to Paris,
share with the present enamel the addition of
applied cast figures on an enamel ground on the
inside.

1. Most completely studied are the Rhenish enamels. (See Guth-Dreyfus 1954.) A small group, comprising mainly objects now in London, has been assigned to England on the basis of stylistic similarities to contemporary English manuscripts and iconographic peculiarities suggesting an English patron. (See Campbell 1980, pp. 418-423.) The largest group of enamels is usually given to Paris, primarily on the basis of stylistic relationships to the illuminated miniatures of the Parisian painter Jean Pucelle or to the few securely localized enamels – i.e., those that are either inscribed (the base of the silver statue of the Virgin presented by Jean d'Evreux to Saint Denis in 1339) or stamped with the Paris hallmark since 1313, the *fleur-de-lis* in a lozenge (a ewer in the Nationalmuseet in Copenhagen, a chalice by Jehan de Toul in Wipperfürth, and an enameled censer in the Strängnäs Cathedral in Sweden; see Paris 1981a, pp. 220-248).

2. See especially the Breviary of Philippe le Bel (Bibliothèque Nationale, Paris, lat. 1023) and *La Somme le Roy* (British Library, London, Add. 54180; see Millar 1959). The authors are grateful to Professor Ellen Kosmer for these comparisons.

3. British Library, London, Royal MS 2.B.vii. See Warner 1912, esp. pp. 147, 148, 163, 212, 228, 260.

4. See Ottawa 1972, p. 146 n. 1; Verdier 1980.

5. The group includes the Copenhagen ewer and the base of the statuette given by Jean d'Evreux mentioned in note 1. See Ottawa 1972, p. 145.

6. Nationalmuseet acc. no. D2304. The chalice comes from the church of Sainte-Marie in Elseneur. See Paris 1968, p. 276, no. 429.

7. Metropolitan Museum, New York, acc. no. 1980.366 (see Cleveland 1967, pp. 192-193, no. VI 2); Musée du Louvre, Paris, acc. no. OA 939 (see Paris 1981a, pp. 247-248, no. 199 bis).

8. Kunsthistorisches Museum, Vienna, acc. no. 8878. See Paris 1981a, pp. 246-247, no. 199; Rossacher 1966, p. 120, no. 15, pl. 7.

39

CONTAINER WITH SAINT JOHN THE BAP-
TIST AND NOLI ME TANGERE
Paris (?), second or third quarter of 14th
century (?)
Crystal or cast glass with gilded silver mounts,
basse-taille enamel and gilding on silver
H: 46 mm. (1 13/16 in.)
DIAM. of base: 36 mm. (1 7/16 in.)
53.2374   *Harriet Otis Cruft Fund*

PROVENANCE: E. Landau, Paris; John Hunt, Dublin

DESCRIPTION: Bowl mounted on a raised foot with
a circular enamel, depicting the *Noli me tangere*,
inserted on the underside. Three hinged bands attach
the foot to a ring around the opening at the top. The
lid consists of a round enamel, showing John the
Baptist, framed by two separate rings. Enamels are
hammered, chased, enameled, and gilded. Enamel colors are opaque red and translucent green, lapis blue,
and purple. John the Baptist, with a green halo (par-
tially cut off by the frame) and dressed in a wide, furry
mauve garment lined in purple, stands on green grass.
The background is lapis-blue with a dotted lozenge
design. In the *Noli me tangere*, Mary Magdalene in a
mauve mantle kneels to the right of Christ with her
hands raised in prayer. The resurrected Christ, with a
red cross inscribed in his gilded halo and wrapped in a
green and mauve mantle, holds a crossed staff in his
right hand. The figures stand on a narrow strip of grass
against a hatched blue ground. The chased details of
the faces and body are filled with the lapis-blue enamel
of the background.

CONDITION: Pristine except for small cracks in the
surface of the enamel.

The figure of John the Baptist on the lid suggests
that the receptacle may have been used for the oil
of the catechumens. The seemingly unrelated
subjects on the two enamels could be explained if
this vessel were part of a series of three for the
holy oils, with the others having related figures
and scenes from the Life of Christ. It is not
impossible, however, that this container served as
a reliquary, as did others of similar construction,
but with conical lids, in Rome,[1] Dijon,[2] and the
Blumka collection in New York.[3] The imprecise
and loose drawing of the present figures
(revealed especially in microphotographs), the
nearly perfect condition of the enamels, and the
presence of chromium[4] in the green enamel raise
doubts about the object's authenticity. Until the
basse-taille enamels produced in each of the European centers have been studied in detail,[5] the
question of authenticity cannot be resolved.

Perhaps closest in style to the present example
is the small folding altar in Vienna with four
scenes from the Passion enameled on the
outside.[6] The two objects share a hatched background, a sketchy rendering of the faces, the
same combination of different types of halos, and
stocky figures dressed in broad drapery with
deep looping folds. The Vienna altar is thought
to be Parisian work of the second or third quarter of the fourteenth century, and thus suggests a
similar provenance and date for the Boston piece,
if it proves to be authentic. If not, the Vienna
altar may have served as the forger's model.

1. In the Lateran Palace, treasury of the Sancta
Sanctorum. See Braun 1940, p. 242, fig. 199.

2. Musée de Dijon. See Dijon 1962, p. 44, no. 88.

3. See New York 1968, no. 139.

4. See p. XXI.

5. See no. 38 n. 1.

6. Kunsthistorisches Museum acc. no. 8878. See Paris
1981a, pp. 246-247, no. 199; Rossacher 1966, p. 120,
no. 15, pl. 7.

40

OVAL PLAQUE WITH SAINT EDMUND AND
ANGELS
England (?), late 14th century (?)
Basse-taille enamel and gilding on silver
H: 62 mm. (2⁷⁄₁₆ in.) W: 51 mm. (2 in.)
63.1249 *Theodora Wilbour Fund in Memory of
Charlotte Beebe Wilbour*

PROVENANCE: Hermann Baer, London

DESCRIPTION: An oval plaque with a circular area
cut out in the center. Hammered, engraved, enameled,
and gilded. Enamel colors are opaque red and translucent lapis blue, green, light blue green, purple (three
shades), apple green, and amber. Clear enamel is also
used. The upper portion of the plaque is divided into a
triple pointed arcade whose red spandrels have green
trefoil windows. The outer sides have wing-like
designs in green and red. At the bottom is a reserved
scroll placed against a lapis-blue ground and flanked by
areas of green with three reserved triangles. Two
angels in long amber tunics with scrolls, upright multicolored wings, and red halos stand in the outer
arches. The angel on the right points to what was
probably a crystal covering a relic in the center. Two
seated music-making angels, with garments composed
of amber tops and skirts of clear enamel, sit below the
central circle. Their multicolored wings conform to the
shape of the circle. Above is a half-figure of Saint
Edmund transfixed by arrows and bound to a tree
draped with a cloth that is apple green on one side and
purple on the other. He is bearded and has a red halo,
a domed purple crown with a clear enamel band at its
base, and a loincloth of clear enamel. The lapis-blue
background has a dotted lozenge pattern; the speckled
groundline is a mixture of blue and clear glasses. The
engraved lines of the hair are filled with amber glass;
the others are filled with the lapis blue of the
background.

CONDITION: The original gilding is almost completely abraded. The enamel is chipped in places and
there is a large loss in the tunic of the angel on the
right. The inscription on the scroll at the bottom has
been scratched out.

This unusually shaped plaque was probably
mounted on a reliquary with a crystal in the
central opening displaying a relic of the saint
represented above, whose name most likely was
inscribed on the scroll below. The saint's crown
identifies him as the East Anglian King Edmund,
rather than Sebastian, the Roman soldier who
was martyred in the same way. According to

legend, Edmund was tied to a tree and shot with
arrows by Danish invaders in 869.[1] He is shown
in two fourteenth-century English manuscripts,
the Queen Mary Psalter[2] and the Carmelite Missal,[3] tied half-naked to a tree, studded with
arrows and surrounded by archers.[4]

The figures, with elongated bodies and linear
faces, are reminiscent of those on an enamel
triptych with scenes from the Passion and Resur-
rection[5] and of those drawn by one of the artists
of the Carmelite Missal from the late fourteenth
century.[6] The seated music-making angels and
the angels bearing scrolls are also found in
English manuscripts of the fourteenth century,
for example, the De Lisle Psalter and the Sherbourne Missal, respectively.[7]

However, the absence of precise stylistic parallels for the figures and the chromium[8] in the
green enamel raise doubts about the authenticity
of the piece. If it proves to be medieval, the
presence of Saint Edmund would indicate
English origin and would make it one of the few
translucent enamels securely localized there.[9] It is
possible that it was made at the monastery dedicated to that saint at Bury.

1. On the legend, see Horstman 1901, pp. 326-327.
The authors are grateful to Kathleen Scott for this
identification.

2. British Library, London, Royal MS 2. B.VII, folio
277. See Warner 1912, pl. 271.

3. British Library add. 29704-5, 44892, folio 160v.
See Rickert 1952, pl. 23a.

4. There is good reason to believe that these English
representations of Saint Edmund anticipated and influ-
enced similar scenes of Saint Sebastian. (See Scott
1982, p. 358 n. 74.) For contemporary representations
of Saint Edmund in English works of various media,
see Campbell 1980, pp. 420 and 423 n. 17.

5. Victoria and Albert Museum, London, acc. no.
M545-1910. See Campbell 1983, pp. 40-41, nos. 31d, 32.

6. Folio 99. See Rickert 1952, pl. 10.

7. This observation was made by Kathleen Scott.
De Lisle Psalter: British Library, London, MS Arundel
83, pt. II, folio 134v. Sherbourne Missal: Alnwick
Castle, p. 47. See Marks and Morgan 1981, pls. 22, 30.

8. On chromium, see p. XXI.

9. See no. 38 n. 1.

41

QUATREFOIL PLAQUE OF CHRIST'S DESCENT INTO LIMBO
Upper Rhineland (?), late 14th century (?)
Basse-taille enamel and gilding on silver
H: 86 mm. (3⁵⁄₁₆ in.) W: 81 mm. (3³⁄₁₆ in.)
48.259   *1948 Purchase Fund*

PROVENANCE: D. Schevitch, Paris (sale, Georges Petit, April 4, 1906, no. 79); Otto H. Kahn, New York; Joseph Brummer, New York

BIBLIOGRAPHY: Guth-Dreyfus 1954, p. 46; *Boston Museum Bulletin* 1957, p. 77, no. 26

DESCRIPTION: Quatrefoil plaque with four pinholes in a silver molded and tooled frame. Hammered, engraved, enameled, and gilded. Enamel colors are translucent green, lapis blue, mauve, ocher, light brown, turquoise, and gray blue. Faces, limbs, and accessories are in reserve, engraved, and filled with lapis-blue enamel. Christ, draped in a mauve mantle lined with turquoise and holding a crossed staff with a banner in his left hand, stands in three-quarter view. He extends his right arm to wrest Adam (in an ocher tunic) from the mouth of hell. Eve's head is visible behind Adam. The mouth of hell comprises a snout, a turquoise mane, and a turquoise webbed foot or leaf at the right. Green grass fills the bottom third of the plaque; the background above it is lapis blue.

CONDITION: The top layer of enamel, especially the brown and blue, is chipped in several places, and the gilding is abraded. The frame is modern.

With its companion piece in New York depicting the Nativity (fig. 21)[1] and others, now lost, representing scenes from the life of Christ, this plaque was probably mounted on the arms of a cross in a manner similar to those showing the same subjects on a Spanish cross of the mid-fourteenth century in Gerona.[2] The style of the figures and the palette are typical of Upper Rhenish enamels and manuscripts. The enamel has been assigned to Basel on the basis of its relationship to manuscripts from that center, but such comparisons are not convincing.[3] Perhaps closest in style to the Boston and New York enamels are those on the earlier Upper Rhenish chalice from Wettingen.[4]

The unusual representation of the mouth of hell[5] and the presence of chromium in the green enamel of both the Boston and New York plaques[6] makes their authenticity questionable.

1. Metropolitan Museum acc. no. 17.190.920. Both plaques are from the Collection of D. Schevitch in Paris (sale, Georges Petit, April 4, 1906, no. 78).

2. Cathedral Museum acc. no. 43. See Gauthier 1972, pp. 238, 398-399, no. 191.

3. See Guth-Dreyfus 1954, p. 46.

4. Abbey Treasury, Mehrerau (Austria). See Gauthier 1972, pp. 407-408, no. 220; Heuser 1974, pp. 195-197, no. 126. The chalice is usually dated to the first half of the fourteenth century.

5. It is possible that this illogical representation of the mouth of hell could result from a forger's misunderstanding of an illustration of the Descent like that found on the engraved silver base of an enamel triptych of the fourteenth century in the Musée Diocesan in Namur (acc. no. 9; see François 1981, fig. 11). Here there is an open mouth of a lion with the snout placed vertically (as in the present representation) and his mane placed along the lower edge. An ivy leaf to the right of the head, an ornamental device used to divide one scene from the next, is in the same position as the webbed foot on the Boston plaque.

6. On chromium see p. xxi. The authors are grateful to Charles Little and the research scientists of the Metropolitan Museum for analyzing the enamel on their plaque.

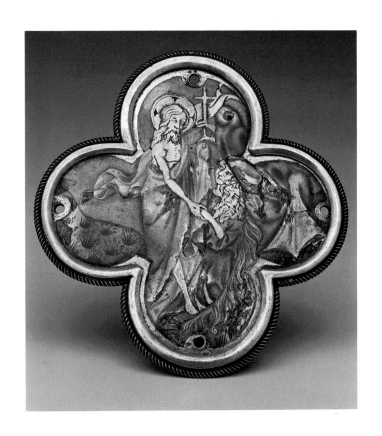

Fig. 21. Quatrefoil Plaque of Nativity.
Metropolitan Museum of Art, New York.

42

ESCUTCHEON OF THE ARTE DELLA LANA
Florence, late 14th century
Champlevé enamel and gilding on copper
H: 118 mm. (4¹¹⁄₁₆ in.) W: 71 mm. (2⅞ in.)
49.489   *William Francis Warden Fund*

PROVENANCE: Ercole Canessa, Naples and New
York, 1957; Joseph Brummer, New York (sale, Parke-
Bernet, May 14, 1949, no. 715)

BIBLIOGRAPHY: *Boston Museum Bulletin* 1957, p. 86,
no. 42; Gauthier 1972, p. 393

EXHIBITIONS: San Francisco 1915, p. 156, no. 160;
New York 1975, no. 156.

DESCRIPTION: Convex shield with an attachment
hole at the top. Hammered, *champlevé*, engraved,
enameled, and gilded. Enamel colors are lapis blue and
red. Against a lapis-blue ground, the Lamb of Christ is
in reserve and engraved. He has red enameled feet and
ears and holds a staff surmounted by a cross, with a
banner displaying a red cross. Arranged horizontally
across the top are four gilded *fleurs-de-lis* within red
niches.

CONDITION: There are losses of enamel near the
outer edges and adjacent to the banner. The original
gilding is almost completely abraded and the halo and
fleurs-de-lis have been regilded.

This is the badge of one of the most prosperous
Florentine guilds, the wool merchants, called the
Arte della Lana. A nearly identical escutcheon is
in the Museo Nazionale di Bargello in Florence.[1]
Suspended from chains around the neck, these
badges were probably worn by messengers em-
ployed by the guild. Other escutcheons of similar
type and also of Florentine origin represent the
pontifical arms (the crossed keys of Saint Peter)[2]
and the symbol of Florence (the red lily).[3]

1. Acc. no. 765. See Gauthier 1972, pp. 229, 393, no. 182.
2. Museo Nationale di Bargello acc. no. 764. See ibid.,
p. 393, no. 182.
3. Musée du Louvre acc. no. OA 6284. See ibid., no.
183.

· 43 ·

Spoon with Fox in Ecclesiastical Garb Preaching to Geese
South Netherlands, ca. 1430
Painted enamel and gilding on silver
H: 176 mm. (6¹⁵⁄₁₆ in.) W: 49 mm. (1¹⁵⁄₁₆ in.)
D: 26 mm. (1 in.)
51.2472 *Helen and Alice Colburn Fund*

PROVENANCE: A. S. Drey, Munich, 1927; Prince of Anhalt-Dessau, Dessau; Baron Max von Goldschmidt-Rothschild, Frankfurt; Rosenberg and Stiebel, New York

BIBLIOGRAPHY: Kohlhaussen 1931, pp. 154-155, figs. 5a, 5b; Bossert 1932, p. 389; Verdier 1956, pp. 29-31, fig. 19; *Boston Museum Bulletin* 1957, p. 86, no. 41; Steingräber 1963, p. 164; Young 1968, pp. 447-449, fig. 9; H. Swarzenski 1969, pp. 492-493, no. 14; Campbell 1983, p. 2

EXHIBITIONS: Detroit 1960, no. 131, pp. 294-296; Bruges 1960, no. 115, p. 217; New York 1975, no. 270, p. 273

DESCRIPTION: The silver spoon is composed of several pieces: a painted enamel bowl with an applied gilded silver edge and central strip on the back; a cast lion head joining the stem and the bowl; a silver stem wound with a gilded silver band to create a spiral field for enamel; and a gilded silver floral finial cast in two pieces. The figures in *grisaille* and the triangular tree-tops and rain in gold are painted over a lapis-blue enamel ground. The stem has traces of green and blue enamel. The fig-shaped bowl appearing to emanate from the mouth of the lion shows, on the inside, a fox standing in a pulpit and wrapped in a monk's habit with three dead geese, whose heads emanate from the cowl. The fox preaches from a charter with a dangling seal (on which only the word "pax" is legible) to a flock of geese who stand on a hillside. Another fox, seated below the pulpit, seizes one of the congregants. Above a fleeing goose is a scroll with an undecipherable inscription. At the top of the scene, on both the front and the back sides of the bowl, golden rain and rays emanate from a small cloud. The back side shows a dense forest of trees on hilly ground.

CONDITION: A small area at the bottom of the inside of the bowl, where the enamel is missing, has been filled with black wax. On the back, some of the enamel was chipped (in an accident in Bruges in 1960) and reattached, and nearly all of the enamel that once covered the stem has disappeared.

Satirizing the clergy as unworthy interpreters of Christianity, the theme of a fox preaching to geese probably derives from the *Van den Vos Reynarde*, a thirteenth-century Flemish poem based on the *Roman de Renart*.[1] The scene, probably originating in drolleries of Gothic manuscripts, shows Renard disguising himself as a preacher in order to gull and capture his prey; it appears commonly in church decoration of the fourteenth and fifteenth centuries, especially on the ends of choir stalls and on misericords.[2]

The spoon belongs to a group of about fifteen objects of similar technique and *grisaille* palette.[3] Within the group, those closest in style to the present example are another spoon of more elongated proportion representing a monkey riding a stag;[4] a cup decorated with a series of apes who, having robbed a sleeping peddler, play with his possessions;[5] a pendant with the *Ara Coeli*;[6] a pair of covered beakers on lion stands;[7] a monstrance with twisted columns;[8] and a double cup known only from a drawing.[9] The Boston spoon shares with them several distinctive features of the landscape: a cloud band issuing golden rays and raindrops, wave-like rocky cliffs, and clumps of trees with slender trunks and triangular tops. The latter may be compared with those painted by Paul de Limbourg about 1415-1416 in the *Très Riches Heures*.[10] With its enamel intact, the handle of the Boston spoon must have resembled the enameled colonnettes of the monstrance mentioned above.

Many of these painted enamels, several of which may have been part of the same table set, are thought to have been made for the Burgundian court of Philip the Good (1419-1467), who adopted the colors of the enamels (black, gray, and white) after the death of his father, John the Fearless, in 1419. Two saltcellars and a goblet, both decorated with *grisaille* enamel, are mentioned in an inventory of Philip the Good's possessions, made after his death in 1467. The enamels are usually assigned to a South Netherlandish workshop in the second quarter of the fifteenth century.[11] In support of this localization,

in an inventory of 1596 from the Castle of Ambras the beakers mentioned above are described as "Niderlenndisch Schmelzwerch"; also, a beaker with white leaf-scrolls on black ground appears in an early-sixteenth-century Netherlandish painting, *The Marriage at Cana*, by Gerard David.[12]

1. On the *Roman de Renart* and its various translations, see Flinn 1963.

2. For other representations of this scene, see Varty 1967, pp. 51-59.

3. On the group, see Kohlhaussen 1931, pp. 153-162; Verdier 1956, pp. 24-37; Steingräber 1963, pp. 147-192.

4. Victoria and Albert Museum, London, acc. no. C2-1935. See Verdier 1956, p. 30.

5. Metropolitan Museum, New York, acc. no. 52.50. (See Young 1968, pp. 441-454.) A cup on which this scene is represented is mentioned as one of nine enamel goblets in the inventory of Piero de Medici from 1465.

6. Walters Art Gallery, Baltimore, acc. no. 44.462. See Verdier 1956, pp. 9-37.

7. Kunsthistorisches Museum, Vienna, acc. nos. 49 and 65. See Fritz 1982, pp. 273, nos. 621-622.

8. Hermitage Museum, Leningrad. See Kohlhaussen 1931, pp. 166-168.

9. Formerly in the Treasury at Halle. The drawing is contained in the Hallesche Heiltumband, an inventory of 1526 preserved in the Aschaffenburg Schlossbibliothek (Man. 14). See Halm and Berliner 1931, pl. 144.

10. Musée Condé, Chantilly, MS 65. See Meiss 1974, pl. 549.

11. For the possibility that some may have been made in Venice, see Steingräber 1963, pp. 159-169, 181-183.

12. See Detroit 1960, pp. 294-296.

enlarged detail

QUATREFOIL PLAQUE WITH ANGEL HOLDING INSTRUMENTS OF THE PASSION

France, mid-15th century

Basse-taille enamel and gilding on silver

H: 63 mm. (2½ in.) W: 62 mm. (2⁷⁄₁₆ in.)

57.741   *John H. and Ernestine A. Payne Fund*

PROVENANCE: Mathias Komor, New York

DESCRIPTION: Thin, roughly cut plaque enameled on both sides. Hammered, engraved, enameled, and gilded. Enamel colors are translucent lapis blue, purple, light gray blue, and deep blue (resulting from a mixture of the lapis-blue and purple glasses). The surface of the silver below the enamel is roughly scored. In the central circle, an angel, holding instruments of the Passion, is in reserve with details engraved and filled with the dark-blue glass of the background. With spread wings following the curve of the circle, the long-haired angel, dressed in a long tunic with wide sleeves, kneels on his left knee and holds a nail in each hand. The quatrefoil shape is defined by a continuous twisted purple band. The back, with shallow hatching in the silver, is covered with gray-blue enamel.

CONDITION: There are considerable losses of enamel on both sides, especially in the twisted band and the right roundel; only traces of the gilding remain on the edges. Radiographs reveal a small circular plug below the enamel under the angel's right wing.

This plaque and two others in the Cluny Museum in Paris (figs. 22 and 23),[1] on which only traces of the enamel remain, come from the same object. Each of the Paris angels rests on one knee; one holds a scroll spread in front of him and the other holds a chalice in his right hand. As they display instruments of the Passion, they were probably mounted on the arms of a cross surrounding a Crucifix. The twisted band defining the roundels, actually a late Roman motif, is unusual for the fifteenth century. The figures, however, with their ovoid heads and voluminous drapery with deep, hatched folds, are reminiscent of those in miniatures of Jean Fouquet, the painter whose style dominated the development of French painting during the second half of the fifteenth century.[2] Comparison with the kneeling angels in a representation of the birth of John the Baptist, in Fouquet's Book of Hours made for Etienne Chevalier between 1452 and 1456, suggests a date for the enamels in the middle of the fifteenth century.[3]

1. Acc. nos. Cl 14721a-b.

2. On Fouquet see, most recently, Paris 1981b.

3. Musée Condé, Chantilly, MS 71. See Perls 1940, pl. 26. Two painted enamels of somewhat different style have been attributed to Fouquet. (See ibid., pls. 44-45.)

Fig. 22. Quatrefoil Plaque with Angel holding a Chalice. *Cluny Museum, Paris.*

Fig. 23. Quatrefoil Plaque with Angel holding a Scroll. *Cluny Museum, Paris.*

TRIPTYCH PENDANT WITH MARTYRDOM OF SAINT BARBARA, MARY MAGDALENE, AND SAINT GEREON

Cologne, 1504
Basse-taille enamel and gilding on silver
H: 72 mm. (2¹³⁄₁₆ in.)
W (open): 63 mm. (2½ in.)
W (closed): 36 mm. (1⅜ in.) D: 9 mm. (⅜ in.)
47.1450 *1941 Purchase Fund*

PROVENANCE: Julia A. Berwind, New York (sale, Parke-Bernet, November 11, 1939, no. 363); Joseph Brummer, New York

BIBLIOGRAPHY: *Boston Museum Bulletin* 1957, p. 91, no. 50

EXHIBITIONS: New York 1975, no. 101, p. 91

DESCRIPTION: Pendant triptych comprising a central box, hinged wings, a predella, and a crowning super-structure. The inside of the wings and the box are enameled with opaque red and translucent red, green, lapis blue, purple, and amber. Both clear and amber enamels are placed over gold foil.

Four arches surmounted by two rows of oval win-dows decorate both the outside of the wings and the inside of the central panel. On the inside, the windows alternate horizontally and vertically between blue and green translucent enamel with the interstices filled with red opaque enamel. A thin gilded plate from which the design has been cut out is laid over the enamel. With an overall engraved dot-and-lozenge pattern, the gilded wings are framed by a simple soldered molding.

A single bent strip forms the sides of the central box onto which is fastened (with two rivets visible on the back) a representation of the beheading of Saint Bar-bara in cast gilded silver. Saint Barbara kneels beside her tower, while her father, dressed as a warrior, raises his sword behind her. Three spiral colonnettes attached to a hilly, engraved ground terminate in branches that intertwine to form the two flat arches framing the scene.

When the triptych is open, Mary Magdalene (on the left) and Saint Gereon (on the right) face the central scene. Both stand within pointed arches against finely hatched blue grounds. These arches, with intricate scrolls over translucent red enamel in the spandrels, are cut from the same plaque as the molding around the edge that is soldered to the enameled plate below. Both figures have gold faces and finely hatched amber halos. Appropriately, Saint Gereon is dressed as a knight. His red mantle with a gilded border is lined in amber, and his blue armor has a short breastplate with a heavy amber collar and a green skirt (imitating satin

or velvet) with a tooled amber border. He wears pointed red shoes and a plumed baret over his long, curly amber hair and carries all of his attributes: a shield, a sword, and a banner. The latter curls behind his head and is seen from the reverse on the right. Mary Magdalene wears a green tunic with long sleeves below a short-sleeved narrow gown of red damask (with its design in gold). It is tied above the waist with a long blue sash decorated with a lozenge-and-dot design. Her mantle is purple with a green lining and her striped turban is green and red.[1] She holds her attribute, an ointment jar (the vessel in one hand and the top in the other) that she used to anoint Christ's feet.

Above a cornice of palmettes and emanating from spiral colonnettes soldered to the sides of the central box are branches with leaves that intertwine and culminate in a central loop. The predella soldered to the base has trefoil openwork designs and a loop attached to the bottom. The date "1504" has been inscribed on the bottom with (as revealed under high magnification) the same pointed tool as the windows on the wings.

CONDITION: Gilding is somewhat abraded, especially on the ground of the Saint Barbara scene, and the heart attached to the lower loop is modern.

Reproducing in miniature Gothic altarpieces with painted wings and sculptural centers, such pendants belong to a type developed in the four-teenth century (see no. 38). Nearly contempo-rary with the present example are two from the late fifteenth century in Cleveland[2] and Paris,[3] both of which are thought to be French.

The central subject of the present example is Saint Barbara. Imprisoned by her father in order to exclude suitors, she persuaded builders to cre-ate a third window in her tower. A priest entered through this opening and baptized her, where-upon she called the three windows symbols of the Trinity. The scene here shows her father, angered by Barbara's conversion, in the act of beheading her. In retribution, her father was struck by lightning, and thus Saint Barbara became the protectress against lightning and sud-den death. As such, she is an appropriate subject for this type of amulet worn around the neck. Saint Barbara was especially revered in Cologne, and often appears with warrior saints. Here, she is shown with Mary Magdalene and Gereon, the

warrior saint of Cologne who was martyred near that city and whose relics are venerated in the church bearing his name. The presence of Saints Barbara and Gereon, then, suggests that the pendant was made in Cologne.

Additional support for this attribution is provided by the figure style, which may be compared to that on contemporary painted altarpieces from Cologne like that showing Saint Gereon in a similar pose by the Master of the Glorification of the Virgin.[4]

The use of foliate scrolls to form arches and the crowning superstructure is a feature found on contemporary German altarpieces.[5] Particularly close to the arches enamating from twisted columns are those on the silver shrine of Saints Gervasius and Protasius made in Strasbourg in 1496.[6]

1. The authors are grateful to Anne H. van Buren for assistance with this description. She believes the old-fashioned (early-fifteenth-century) costumes are customary for representations of saints at this later date.

2. Cleveland Museum of Art acc. no. 47.508. See Cleveland 1967, pp. 322-323, 385, no. VII 15.

3. Musée du Louvre acc. no. OA 5568. See Evans 1953, p. 79, pl. 34a.

4. Wallraf-Richartz Museum, Cologne, acc. no. WRM120. See Reiners 1925, pp. 106-110, pl. 114. The topography of Cologne in the background suggests a date for the painting after 1493.

5. For example, the altarpiece by Tilman Riemenschneider in Creglingen from about 1505-1510. See Baxandall 1980, p. 65, pl. 27.

6. In Münster St. Stephen, Breisach. See Fritz 1982, p. 283, pls. 705-707.

BUCKLE PLATE
Northern France, Belgium or Rhineland, ca.
480-520
Glass, gilded silver cloisons, tin, silver foil, and
iron
W: 42 mm. (1¾ in.) H: 29 mm. (1³⁄₁₆ in.)
D: 8 mm. (³⁄₈ in.)
60.122   *Gift of Leopold Blumka*

PROVENANCE: Leopold Blumka, New York

BIBLIOGRAPHY: Brown 1984, p. 22, fig. 14

DESCRIPTION: Kidney-shaped iron buckle plate with
silver cloisons arranged in a symmetrical geometric
design. The cloisons are soldered to a tin plate that is
attached to the iron base with three pins. Between the
cloisons are green, deep orange, and red translucent
glass over silver foil.

CONDITION: Traces of gold indicate that the cloisons
were gilded. The glass is cracked in several places and
the iron base is corroded on the back. There are solder
repairs on the upper left edge, and the silver foil is
tarnished in several places.

Commonly found in the graves of Frankish mili-
tary chiefs datable between 480 and 520, such
plates belong with either oval or rectangular
buckles that are often decorated with similar *cloisonné* designs.[1] Close in style to the present example is a complete buckle found in the Merovin-
gian Necropolis at Lavoye, France.[2] Others have
been found in France at Anguilcourt-le-Sart,
Arcy-Sainte-Restitue, Marchélepot, and
Mézières; in Belgium at Haillot and Samson; and
in Germany at Schwarzrheindorf and Bingen.[3]

1. See Brown 1984, p. 22.
2. See Joffroy 1974, pp. 95-96, fig. 72.
3. See ibid; Werner 1966, pp. 283-292.

47

CIRCULAR BROOCH
Italy, first half of 7th century
Gold and colored glass
DIAM.: 48 mm. (1¹⁵⁄₁₆ in.)
59.13   *Edwin E. Jack Fund*

PROVENANCE: Sir Thomas Gibson Carmichael, London (sale, Christie's, May 13, 1902, no. 189); Marc Rosenberg, Baden-Baden (sale, Graupe-Ball, Berlin, November 4, 1929, no. 120); L. Burg, London; Otto Wertheimer, Paris

BIBLIOGRAPHY: Rosenberg 1911, p. 331, fig. 6; Rosenberg 1918, p. 43, fig. 58; Von Falke 1929, pp. 416-417

DESCRIPTION: The brooch is made of a circular gold plate with soldered gold cloisons filled with glass on the front and a twisted cable around the edge. Cloisons form a central rosette with eight green petals surrounded by three concentric bands. The innermost of the bands has rectangular cells filled with alternating red, green, white, and yellow glasses. The second is composed of triangular sections of alternating blue and millefiori glasses, and the outer band is a series of empty curved cells. On the back are soldered two gold rings to hold the pin and a curved piece of gold decorated with filigree to serve as the catch. A third loop, probably used at a later date for suspending the brooch, is modern.

CONDITION: The outer cells may have been filled with pearls. Glass insets are missing from three of the inner cells, and the pin is lacking on the back.

Derived from Roman millefiori fibulae,[1] the present brooch is comparable to several found in Langobard graves of the first half of the seventh century. Of similar size, construction, and design are two circular brooches in Rome from which the glass insets are now missing.[2] The placement of the pin in a central position on the back and the filigree circles on the catch are typical of Langobard goldsmiths' work.[3] Roman millefiori glass may have been reused here.

1. See, for example, Cologne 1981, pp. 38-39, nos. 11-12.
2. Museo dell'Alto Medioevo. See Werner 1950, pp. 34-35, nos. C4 (excavated at Nocera Umbra) and C6 (excavated at Castel Trosino). The authors are grateful to Renate Eikelmann for this comparison.
3. See Werner 1950, pls. 36(C4), 37(C5), and 42.

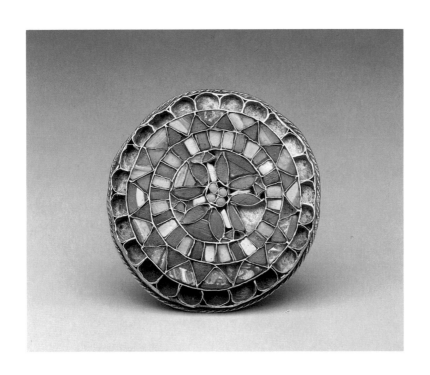

48

MEDALLION WITH SAINT SOPHIA
Venice, first half of 13th century
Glass paste
H: 26 mm. (1 7/16 in.) W: 20 mm. (7/8 in.)
40.727 *Samuel Putnam Avery Fund*

PROVENANCE: Kirkor Minassian, New York

BIBLIOGRAPHY: Wentzel 1957, p. 65, no. 31

DESCRIPTION: Opaque red molded medallion with a half-length frontal figure of Saint Sophia inscribed on either side H A[ΓΙΑ] CОФІА. With her right hand raised in benediction, she wears a tunic and mantle and a veil covering her head. Her nimbus consists of a series of dots.

CONDITION: There is iridescence on the surface resulting from decomposition of the glass. Where the iridescence has flaked off pitting occurs.

Thought to imitate more valuable carved gems, these glass-paste medallions were made in large quantity by pressing a mold over opaque or transparent molten glass. Nearly two hundred such cameos from about sixty different molds have been recorded.[1] Their homogeneity in style and technique suggest their production in a single center. Almost all represent sacred subjects, either scenes from the lives of Christ and the Virgin or saints, and many have either Latin or Greek inscriptions. Both their iconography and their wide distribution suggest that they were pilgrims' mementoes.

The question of whether this large group of molded medallions is Byzantine or Italian has been much debated. Because so many have been found in the East and are similar to Byzantine seals, the group has been assigned to Constantinople and has been dated variously in the eleventh, twelfth, and thirteenth centuries.[2] More convincing, however, are the arguments attributing the group to Venice in the thirteenth century on several grounds: (1) many of the motifs have parallels only in Western art; (2) the Byzantine iconography and style found on one group of

medallions would not be out of place in Venice in this period; (3) many have modern Venetian provenance; and (4) glass technology was highly developed in Venice at this time.[3] Analysis of the opaque glasses used in a number of these medallions preserved in the British Museum offers additional support for Venetian origin. All of the opaque medallions were found to be composed of the same three colored glasses (dark purple, red-orange, and black) mixed in varying proportions. Although red-orange glass is rarely found in Constantinople, it is common in Italian mosaics.[4]

The present medallion with Sophia, rarely depicted in this period, is the only one known from this mold, but there are six others from a different mold (three in Berlin and one each in Edinburgh, Athens, and London[5]) with the same, if slightly wider, image of this saint. Depictions of Sophia usually show her with her daughters, Hope, Faith, and Charity, and as a nun or a Byzantine matron with a crown.[6] On the basis of their Eastern iconography, facial types, and drapery, the medallions are assigned to a "Byzantinizing" group of the first half of the thirteenth century.[7]

1. See the catalogue in Wentzel 1957, pp. 64-67; additions in Wentzel 1963, pp. 17-18; and Vickers 1974, pp. 18-20.

2. See Ross 1962, pp. 87-91.

3. See Wentzel 1957, pp. 50-63; Wentzel 1963, pp. 17-24. For a summary of his arguments see Vickers 1974, p. 21.

4. See Buckton 1981, pp. 187-188.

5. Bode Museum, Berlin, acc. nos. 764, 2541, and 6399; Collection of David Talbot Rice, Edinburgh; Benaki Museum, Athens, acc. no. 55; British Museum, London, acc. no. 1934.11-9.1.

6. See *Lexikon* 1968-1976, cols. 382-384; De Tervarent 1950, pp. 419-423.

7. See Wentzel 1963, p. 21.

135

49

MEDALLION WITH SAINT NICHOLAS
Venice, second half of 13th century
Opaque red glass paste
H: 24 mm. (1 in.) W: 18 mm. (13/16 in.)
40.728 *Samuel Putnam Avery Fund*

PROVENANCE: Kirkor Minassian, New York

BIBLIOGRAPHY: Wentzel 1957, p. 67, no. 43;
London 1979, p. 14

DESCRIPTION: Opaque red molded medallion with a
half-length frontal figure of Saint Nicholas inscribed
on either side O A[ΓIOC] NHKOΛAOC in relief. His
right arm is raised in a gesture of benediction.
He has closely cropped hair, balding on top, and
a short beard. Dressed as an Eastern bishop, he
wears a pallium. The nimbus is a continuous line.

CONDITION: The medallion is chipped at the top.

The present example representing Saint
Nicholas, the fourth-century bishop of Myra
whose relics were enshrined at Bari in 1087, is
one of eleven known to be from the same mold.
Others are in London, New York, Edinburgh,
Berlin, Venice, Istanbul, Toronto, Rome, and
Leningrad,[1] and one was formerly in the collection of Jean Lambros in Athens. Some examples,
like that in London,[2] show the saint holding a
book in his draped left hand. Thus, the mold was
cut back, replacing the book with folded drapery
inconsistent with the saint's costume, before the
Boston medallion was made. On the basis of the
facial type and proportions of the figure, the
Saint Nicholas medallions fall within the so-
called Saint Anne Group, dated to the second
half of the thirteenth century.[3]

1. British Museum acc. no. 93,4-9,3; Metropolitan
Museum acc. no. 18.145.9; collection of David Talbot
Rice; Bode Museum acc. no. 6400; Museo Correr acc.
no. 541; Archaeological Museum acc. no. 4960; Royal
Ontario Museum, A. Kann collection; collection of A.
Canessa; Hermitage. See Wentzel 1957, p. 67, no 43;
Wentzel 1963, p. 18.

2. See London 1979, p. 14, fig. e.

3. See Wentzel 1963, p. 21, and above no. 48.

· 50 ·

MEDALLION WITH SAINTS PETER AND
PAUL
Venice, second half of 13th century
Glass paste
H: 21 mm. (⅞ in.) W: 16 mm. (¹¹⁄₁₆ in.)
40.730   *Samuel Putnam Avery Fund*
PROVENANCE: Kirkor Minassian, New York
BIBLIOGRAPHY: Wentzel 1957, p. 65, no. 32

DESCRIPTION: Translucent green molded medallion
representing the Adoration of the Cross in relief.
Flanking the cross, Peter and Paul stand on a
groundline with their inner arms raised. Two reversed
*P*s appear above the figures' heads. On the left, Paul
with a pointed beard holds a sword, the instrument of
his Passion, in his right arm. On the right, Peter has
short hair and a closely cropped beard and holds keys,
the ends of which have been broken off. The nimbi are
a continuous line.

CONDITION: The faces are rubbed, the glass is
chipped on the right side and at the bottom, and there
is a horizontal crack near the bottom.

No other medallion from this mold is known.
Although the translucent medallions have most
recently been ascribed to Constantinople on the
basis of their relationship to Byzantine hardstone
cameos,[1] the Western subject and the Latin letters leave little doubt that this medallion should
be assigned to Venice. The figure style is related
to those in the so-called Saint Anne Group of the
second half of the thirteenth century.[2]

1. Buckton 1981, pp. 187-188.
2. See no. 48 and Wentzel 1963, p. 21.

Two Eglomisé plaques with Saint John and Saint Luke

Italy, Venice (?) last third of 13th century
Glass with gold leaf and paint

1974.481   W: 33 mm. (1¹⁵⁄₁₆ in.)
H: 37 mm. (1⁷⁄₁₆ in.)

1974.482   W: 36 mm. (1³⁄₈ in.)
H: 39 mm. (1½ in.)

1974.481-482   *Anonymous Gift in Memory of Georg Swarzenski*

PROVENANCE: Robert Forrer, Strasbourg; Georg Swarzenski, Boston

EXHIBITIONS: Boston 1940, pp. 62-63, nos. 208-209

DESCRIPTION: Two clear glass plaques decorated on the back with half-length figures in three-quarter view. The figures, borders, and roundels containing inscriptions are gold. Blue paint is used for the background.

The mourning Saint John the Baptist has a fragmentary inscription beginning HOC in the roundels on either side. He turns to the left with hands raised. The lines of the head are brown; those of the garment are green.

Luke, inscribed in roundels on either side O ΛΟΥΚΑϹ turns to the right. Brown paint has been placed over the gold to color the lines of the face, short hair, and beard. His tunic is modeled with green lines; the pallium has red lines.

CONDITION: The gold and paint have flaked off in large areas on both plaques, especially on Saint John's face.

Gold leaf drawing behind glass is known as *verre églomisé*, a name derived from the Parisian craftsman Jean-Baptiste Glomy (d. 1786), who revived the technique in the eighteenth century. In the process, gold leaf is pasted to the back of transparent glass and engraved with a fine needle. Paint of various colors is then applied to color the engraved lines and the background where gold has not been applied.[1] The largest group of *églomisé* plaques is Italian and datable to the fourteenth century, yet there are a few examples, like the present plaques, whose style suggests a date in the last third of the thirteenth century.[2] Significant differences in style among the extant plaques indicate that they were made in several Italian centers; the Byzantinizing style and Greek inscriptions of the present pieces imply Venetian origin. In the inventory of Pope Boniface VIII of 1295 is mention of an icon "*de opere Veneticorum*" with figures "*in vitro aurum*,"[3] suggesting that the technique was known in Venice by the end of the thirteenth century. The only other *églomisé* plaques with figures assigned to Venice in the thirteenth century are the two roundels with busts of Saints Mark and John found in the tomb of the French Pope Clement IV (d. 1268).[4] Their attribution is based on the metal mounts, however, and not on the figural style, which has little in common with that of the present plaques.

The Boston pieces, like many *églomisé* examples, were probably mounted on a wooden reliquary. Saint John may have flanked a central crucifix and Saint Luke may have formed part of an outer frame consisting of busts of saints, perhaps alternating with labels of the relics.[5]

1. The technique is described by Cennino d'Andrea Cennini in *Il libro dell'arte* (see Thompson 1933, pp. 107-108). For discussion of the technique and extant examples, see Toesca 1908, pp. 247-261; Rossi 1929, pp. 707-714; G. Swarzenski 1940, pp. 55-68.

2. For thirteenth-century examples, see G. Swarzenski 1926a, p. 326; Bertelli 1970a, pp. 70-78; Bertelli 1973b, pp. 71-80.

3. See Molinier 1888, p. 77, no. 722.

4. Known to the authors only from photographs. See Bertelli 1969, p. 59.

5. For related examples see G. Swarzenski 1940, figs. 4, 7-10.

· 52 ·

SEVEN GLASS PLAQUES
Italy, Venice (?), late 13th century (?)
Glass with gold leaf and lead borders

1973.683 *Saint Paul*
W: 25 mm. (1 in.) H: 60 mm. (2⅜ in.)

1973.684 *Saint Mary Salome*
W: 47 mm. (1⅞ in.) H: 30 mm. (13⁄16 in)

1973.685 *Saint Mary Magdalene*
W: 48 mm. (1¹⁵⁄16 in.) H: 29 mm. (2⅜ in.)

1973.686 *Lion of Saint Mark*
W: 25 mm. (1 in.) H: 29 mm. (1⅛ in.)

1973.687 *Annunciation*
W: 61 mm. (2⅜ in.) H: 49 mm. (1¹⁵⁄16 in.)

1973.688 *Virgin and Child*
W: 47 mm. (1¹⁵⁄16 in.) H: 58 mm. (2⅜ in.)

1973.689 *Nativity*
W: 62 mm. (2⁷⁄16 in.) H: 42 mm. (1⅞ in.)

1973.683-689 *Gift of John Goelet in Honor of Hanns Swarzenski*

PROVENANCE: Prince Esterhazy, Galanta; Wildenstein and Company, New York

BIBLIOGRAPHY: Bertelli 1970, p. 76 n. 15; Bertelli 1973a, p. 68

DESCRIPTION: The plaques representing the Nativity, Saint Paul standing in three-quarter view (inscribed: s PAULUS), and a half-length frontal figure of Saint Mary Magdalene (inscribed:.SCA MARIA MADALENA) are on purple glass. Those depicting the Annunciation, the Virgin and Child (of the Hodegetria type) under an arch (inscribed MH[TH]P θ[EO]Y), a half-length frontal figure of Saint Mary Salome (SCA MARIA SALOME), and the lion of Saint Mark are on dark-blue glass. The decoration and inscriptions are acid-etched, giving a rough, silvery surface to the glass. Gold leaf, in which modeling lines have been scratched, is applied on the front of the glass over the inscriptions, the framing gold bands, the hair and headdresses, the animals, and parts of the architecture and drapery (usually mantles). Thus, the designs depend on the interplay between the etched and gilded surfaces and are read best when placed against a dark ground.

CONDITION: Small areas of gold have flaked off, especially on the inscriptions and framing bands. Each plaque is set in a modern lead frame.

The size, shape, and iconography of the plaques suggest that they, and others now missing, decorated the inside of a reliquary diptych. There are several such Italian diptychs of the fourteenth century with *églomisé* glass.[1] The shape of the present Annunciation and Nativity plaques indicates their placement in the pointed arches of the wings. The plaque showing the Virgin and Child and one now missing (perhaps with a Crucifixion or Enthroned Christ) may have been set in the center of the wings surrounded by rectangular frames in which the remaining four plaques and others alternated with the inserted relics.

Different from the more common *églomisé*,[2] the technique of the present etched and gilded glass is recorded only on a small group of plaques of similar size. They are found on the miter of Saint Raniero in Civita di Bagno,[3] on a Venetian chalice in the Victoria and Albert Museum in London,[4] and on Venetian reliquaries in the Monastery of Ayou Paylou on Mount Athos[5] and the Musée Cinquantenaire in Brussels.[6] Four plaques with scenes from the Life of Christ formerly in the collection of Countess Sierstorpff in Eltville were destroyed in the last war,[7] and two lozenge-shaped plaques are in the British Museum in London.[8]

Given the rarity of the technique, it is surprising that all of the extant examples display somewhat different styles. Although several have been assigned to Venice, precise parallels in Venetian painting have not been identified.[9] In general, the Byzantinizing style of the present plaques may be compared to that of the painted miniatures on the diptych of King Andrew III of Hungary, made in Venice between 1290 and 1296.[10]

The authenticity of the whole group of plaques is questionable, as the accepted date for the introduction of acid etching is about 1670,[11] and there are no recorded examples of the technique before that date. A Bolognese manuscript of 1410-1450, however, contains a recipe for a mixture of three "waters" to etch glass.[12] Thus, it is possible that acid etching on glass was practiced, albeit not widely, in northern Italy at the end of the thirteenth century.

1. See G. Swarzenski 1940, pp. 55-68.

2. For a description of this technique, see no. 51.

3. See Bertelli 1973a, pp. 64-71.

4. Acc. no. 779.1891. The chalice may be the one in a watercolor by Jan Grevembroch about 1760 (in *Varie Venete Curiosità*, Museo Correr, Venice, MS Gradenijo-Dolfin, 219/II, coll. 65, c.xxx; see Hahn-loser 1971, p. 150, pl. 136). Only two lozenge-shaped plaques are clearly visible in this illustration and neither corresponds to any preserved.

5. See Huber 1969, pl. 158; Bertelli 1970, p. 76 n. 15.

6. Acc. no. 3225. See Jansen 1964, p. 26, no. 103; G. Swarzenski 1926b, p. 15.

7. See G. Swarzenski (1926b, pp. 13-16), who describes these plaques and those on the reliquary in Brussels as having been scribed and then silvered in some areas and gilded in others. If, however, the glass was not examined under magnification, the acid-etched surface could easily have been mistaken for silver leaf.

8. Acc. nos. 60.9-28.29-30. These plaques representing the Virgin and Saint Simon are closely related to those on the chalice in the Victoria and Albert Museum (see note 4).

9. See G. Swarzenski 1926b, pp. 14-15; Bertelli 1970, p. 76 n. 15.

10. Historisches Museum, Bern, acc. no. 301. See Maurer 1954, pp. 255-278.

11. See Cassebaum 1983, pp. 213-214; Charleston 1980, pp. 31-39.

12. See Merrifield 1849, vol. 2, pp. 332-333, 494-495. The description of the technique is as follows: "*A fare aqua da tagliare el vetrio. Tolli vitriolo che nasce per le mura et fanne aqua a lambico et serbala bene turata poi tolli vitriolo romano et pistalo bene et fanne aqua a lambico et serbala bene turata poi tolli sale armoniaco et fanne aqua alo lambico et serbala bene et quando la voraj operare tolli de le ditte aque de omne una tanto et mistale insiemj et disegna lo vetrio cum dita aqua et tagliarasse dove sera bagnato cum dita aqua a tuo piacere.*"

enlarged detail

· 53 ·

EGLOMISÉ PLAQUE WITH APOSTLE
Italy, 14th century
Glass with gold leaf and paint
W: 28 mm. (1⅛ in.) H: 98 mm. (3⅞ in.)
1974.483 *Anonymous Gift in memory of Georg Swarzenski*

PROVENANCE: Cologne; Robert Forrer, Strasbourg; Georg Swarzenski, Boston

BIBLIOGRAPHY: Forrer 1893, p. 20, pl. XIII, 18

EXHIBITIONS: Boston 1940, p. 63, no. 210

DESCRIPTION: A clear glass plaque decorated on the back with a half-length saint in gold. He holds a book in his left hand and his head, with short hair and beard, is turned to the left. Above and below are stylized gold palmettes and twisted bands forming arcs that join the rectangular frame to enclose the Apostle. Dark-brown paint has been placed over the gold of the figure to color the modeling lines. Blue and red paint are used for the background.

CONDITION: The edges of the glass are chipped in several places. Areas of the gold frame have flaked off, as has much of the paint.

This plaque belongs with another of slightly smaller size representing a similar figure in reverse.[1] Like the previous examples (nos. 51 and 52), these too were probably mounted on a reliquary diptych and formed part of a frame around a central plaque. They probably date from the fourteenth century, when large quantities of *églomisé* glass of varying quality were produced in many centers.[2] The style, however, is provincial and thus difficult to localize more precisely.

1. Present location unknown. See Forrer 1893, pl. XIII, 17.
2. See G. Swarzenski 1940, p. 57, figs. 6-10.

143

WINDOW WITH EIGHT APOSTLES
England, West Country, 1420-1435
Pot-metal glass, flashed glass, and white glass
with silver-oxide stain
Window – H: 5.63 m. (8 ft., 8 in.)
W: 2.63 m. (8 ft., 8 in.)
Main lights – H: 4.14 m. (13 ft., 6 in.)
W: 48 cm. (19 in.)
25.213 *Maria Antoinette Evans Fund*

PROVENANCE: Hereford Cathedral (?); Hampton
Court, Herefordshire; Wilfred Drake and Grosvenor
Thomas, London, 1924-1925

BIBLIOGRAPHY (Manuscripts): George Coningsby,
"Notes," ca. 1725, in the possession of Lady Mary
Clive; James Hill of the Middle, "Notes," vol. 5, Hereford City Library, folio 339; Bird, "Herefordiane,"
vol. 1, folio 389; R. Grosvenor Thomas, typescript,
1924, Museum of Fine Arts, Boston; (printed
sources): Dingley 1867, pp. 35 (n. 3), 92, pl. 238;
Robinson 1873, p. 145; Karnaghan 1928, p. 100, ill.
p. 98; Skinner 1933, pp. 173-176; Sowers 1965, fig.
9; Caviness 1970, pp. 35-60; Cornforth 1973, p. 584;
Mezey 1979, pp. 8-9; Caviness 1985, pp. 44-45

EXHIBITIONS: Cambridge 1978, pp. 53-55, nos. 22-
23

DESCRIPTION: The glass, now in modern stonework
designed after measured drawings from Hampton
Court, consists of four large perpendicular lights with
trefoil tops, three rectangular tracery lights with pro-
trusions at the top and bottom, and six small triangular
tracery openings. The main lights show eight Apostles
arranged in two rows. Each Apostle stands on a dais
between the shafts of a canopy above. There is an extra
row of canopies at the bottom. In three-quarter view,
the Apostles, who seem to be based on two cartoons,[1]
turn to different sides. They hold attributes, and above
their heads are long scrolls with inscriptions from their
Creed. They stand against blue or red grounds with
acanthus scrolls resembling seaweed in reserve. Their
tunics are blue or red; clear glass with paint and silver
stain is used for their heads, mantles, halos, attributes,
and canopies. From left to right, beginning with the
top row, the Apostles are:

Name	Inscription	Attributes	Passage of Creed
Peter	SC PETRUS	keys, book	CREDO I[N] DEU[M] OM[N]IPO[T]ENTEM CREATORE[M] CELI ET TER[R]E
Andrew	missing	saltire, book	ET IN IH[ESU]M XP[ISTU]M FILIU[M] E[I]US UNICU[M] DOMINU[M] NOS[TRUM]
James Major	S IACOBS	staff, book, hat, and purse with scallop shell, hair garment	Q[U]I CONCEPTUS DE SP[IRIT]U SANCTO NATUS EX MARIA VIR[GINE]
John	JOHES	demon, chalice	PASSUS SUB PONTIO P[ILA]TO [C]RUCI[FIX]US MORTU[U]S ET SEPULTUS
Bartholomew	SCS BARTHOLOMES	flaying knife, book	ASCENDIT AD CELOS SEDET AD DEXT[ER]AM DEI PAT[R]IS OM[N]IPOTE[N]TIS
Matthias	SCS MATHIAS	spear, book	INDE VE[N]TURUS E[ST] IUDICARE IVOS ET MOR[TUOS]
James Minor	S IACOBS	halberd	S[AN]C[T]AM ECCLICIA[M] CATHOLICAM S[AN]C[T]OR[UM] COM[M]UNIONE[M]
Simon	SYMO	oar (?), book	REMISSIONEM PECCATORUM

145

In the three tracery lights are figures represented under fragmentary canopies: Pieta (center), Saint John the Baptist wearing a hair coat with a camel's head (left; inscribed s[an]c[tu]s ioh[annes] baptista), and Saint Francis showing the stigmata (right; inscribed s[an]c[tus] franciscus). The grounds are blue or red with acanthus, and the figures are colored by silver stain, except for Saint Francis, whose robe is painted brown. In the small triangular openings are frontal busts of angels in grisaille.

CONDITION: The window is part of a larger one; the main lights and rectangular tracery lights have been cut down, releaded, and repaired with glass from other parts of the original window. One of the frontal angels is damaged.

The present window is part of one removed in 1924 from a small chapel at Hampton Court near Leominster. Smaller fragments from the same chapel are now in the Victoria and Albert Museum in London; the National Museum of American Art in Washington, D.C.; the north transept of Hereford Cathedral; the Burrell Collection in Glasgow; the Abbey of Saint John, Westmont, near Montreal; and the collection of Dr. and Mrs. Verne Caviness in Lexington, Massachusetts.[2] All have been attributed to a single atelier that was closely allied to those responsible for the Passion Window in Great Malvern Priory Church (ca. 1423-1439) and some of the glass at York Minster including the Saint William window (ca. 1421-1423). Indeed, at least one painter seems to have worked on both the Saint William window and the Hampton Court glass.

Four Apostles and their passages of the Creed are missing, but the tops of their canopies are preserved at the bottom of the present main lights. Given that the canopies over the Boston Apostles have been cut down and that the original window would have had six main lights of larger size and not the five of the present size at Hampton Court, it has been suggested that the glass was commissioned for another building, possibly for the west window of Hereford Cathedral, where the original glass has been replaced. The first record of the glass at Hampton Court is 1683, but when it was installed is unknown.[3]

As reconstructed, the original Creed window would have had high canopies above the figures. The backgrounds of the six main lights would have alternated between red and blue, except in the two central lights, and the figures would have been arranged in facing pairs on the ends and turning away from each other in the center. The smaller Boston lights may have been part of the tracery for the original Creed window or may come from another, smaller window.[4]

1. See Caviness 1970, p. 36.

2. See ibid., pp. 35-60, on which the discussion in this entry is based. The glass formerly in the collection of Dirk de Leur is now in the Burrell Collection; that formerly at Hampton Court is now in the Abbey of Saint John. The location of that formerly in the McConnell Collection is unknown.

3. See ibid., pp. 52-55.

4. See ibid., esp. pl. 31.

The authors are grateful to Madeline Caviness for assistance with this entry.

147

detail

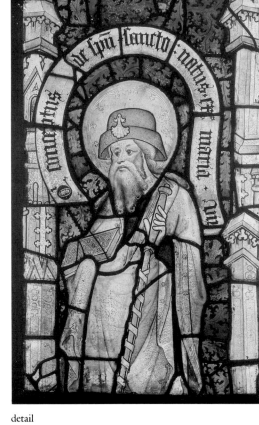

detail

MEDALLION WITH BUST OF SAINT
NICHOLAS
Russia, late 19th century – 1911
Cloisonné enamel on gold
DIAM.: 100 mm. (4 in.)
28.243 *Maria Antoinette Evans Fund*

PROVENANCE: M. P. Botkine, St. Petersburg; E. and
A. Silbermann, New York

BIBLIOGRAPHY: Botkine 1911, pl. 73; Hawes 1928,
pp. 56-57; Siple 1928, p. 198

This is one of about two hundred *cloisonné*
plaques in the Byzantine style assembled at the
end of the nineteenth century by the Russian
collector M. P. Botkine.[1] Although most have
not been examined in detail, many of the enamels
are thought to have been made for him.[2] The
present plaque belongs to a group of nine of
similar size, shape, and style, showing busts of
Saints Peter, Paul, Nicholas, Andrew, Matthew,
Bartholomew, Mark, John Chrysostom, and
Michael.[3] Nicholas, on this example, is represented nearly identically on two enamels belonging to other groups in the Botkine collection,
both with green enameled backgrounds.[4]

The thinness of the *cloisons* and the precision of
the lines formed by them are matched only in

other Botkine enamels – a circumstance leading
to the speculation that a single modern collector
could well have possessed all the existing examples with these distinguishing characteristics.

Other condemning features are the lack of
abrasion on the surface of the enamel, the presence of uranium in the yellow and both chromium and uranium in the green,[5] and the
absence of the usual depressions on the reverse
side of the plaque, where the *cloisons* have been
attached. Indeed, microscopic examination of
areas in which enamel is missing reveals that the
cloisons are attached with clear glass and not
soldered to the base – a technique that has not
been documented on genuine Byzantine
enamels.[6]

---

1. Most of them were published prior to their sale by
Botkine in 1911.
2. See Kurz 1948, pp. 216-218; Washington 1981,
pp. 28-29.
3. See Botkine 1911, pls. 73-75.
4. Ibid., pls. 72, 83.
5. On chromium and uranium see pp. xix and xxii. The
gold contains 1.45 percent copper and 6.40 percent
silver.
6. This observation was made by David Buckton.

149

HANAP
Cologne, workshop of Gabriel Hermeling (?),
second half of 19th century
Silver with gilding and translucent *champlevé*
enamel on silver
H: 136 mm. (5⅜ in.) DIAM. (top): 89 mm. (3½
in.) DIAM. (foot): 100 mm. (3⁵⁄₁₆ in.)
56.101   *Theodora Wilbour Fund in memory of
Charlotte Beebe Wilbour*

PROVENANCE: Clara Bischoffsheim, London; A. &
R. Ball, New York

BIBLIOGRAPHY: Heuser 1959, pp. 215-220; Ottawa
1972, pp. 140-141, no. 55, pl. 77; Heuser 1974, pp.
40-41

This *hanap* has been published as a French work
of the late thirteenth century, but recent examination of its shape, enamels, stamp, and engraved
decoration suggests otherwise. Its wide bowl
with a deep, straight rim and its stem with a
single inset band and no knop are both without
parallel among medieval drinking cups, and thus
raise doubts about the object's authenticity.
Equally unusual for the middle ages are the use
of translucent enamels in silver *champlevé*
grounds,[1] the sprays of flowers with five petals in
the teardrop-shaped enamels, and the motif of
semicircles with three holes forming a triangle on
the cup's upper rim, stem, and base. Indeed, the
flowers are matched on a chessboard in the Victoria and Albert Museum in London, purchased
from the dealer Louis Marcy and attributed to
his workshop of the late nineteenth century, the
location of which is still unknown.[2] The mark on
the *hanap's* rim with the maker's name in Gothic
letters, JEH/SA, bears no resemblance to authentic
marks of the middle ages,[3] but does appear on a
silver shrine in the Metropolitan Museum in
New York,[4] unrelated in style to the present
object and thought to be one of a large group of
forgeries associated with the dealer Louis Marcy.
A similarly suspicious mark, the Gothic letter O,
is found on the base of a chalice in the Oberlin
Museum, which resembles the Boston cup in
shape and decoration and whose authenticity has
also been questioned.[5] Finally, technical analyses
reveal chromium in the green enamel.[6]

The base of the *hanap*, engraved with palmettes emanating from the trefoil arches and
inset with teardrop-shaped enamels, is so similar
to that of an early-fourteenth-century chalice in
the Cathedral Treasury at Mainz[7] that there can
be little doubt that the latter served as the
forger's model. The workshop of the goldsmith
Gabriel Hermeling of Cologne restored this chalice in 1865 and at the same time probably made
the modern chalice in the Church of Saint Gereon in Cologne,[8] the design of whose base also
depends on the Mainz chalice. The enameled
birds on the *hanap* could have been copied from
those on a fourteenth-century bishop's staff in
the Cathedral Treasury in Cologne[9] after which
Hermeling executed a similar staff in the same
treasury.[10] It may be, then, that the Boston cup is
also a product of the Hermeling workshop. If so,
there remains to be explored the possible relationship between this Cologne workshop and the
dealer Louis Marcy.

1. Gothic translucent enamels are normally *basse-taille*,
thereby taking advantage of the enamels' transparency.
For this technique see p. XIX.
2. Louis Marcy established himself in London about
1893, and sold many spurious medieval and Renaissance objects to various collectors. The variety of techniques found in his objects suggests either one very
large workshop or several small ones in different loca-
tions. See Blair and Campbell 1983, pp. 70-73, with
additional bibliography.
3. On these marks, see Rosenberg 1928; Lightbown
1978, pp. 6-9, 91-92, 97-99, 105.
4. Acc. no. 55.1. On the question of authenticity, see
the note by Erich Steingräber in the Museum's file.
5. Allen Memorial Art Museum acc. no. 60.35. Gift of
Melvin Guttman. A letter from John Hayward in the
Museum's file suggests that the piece is a product of
the Marcy workshop.
6. On chromium see p. xxi. The silver previously
reported as 90 percent pure is, in fact, 97.3 percent
pure, the only alloy being copper (2.7 percent).
7. Acc. no. D2. See Cologne 1981, p. 74, nos. 35, 35a.
8. Ibid., pp. 198-199, no. 112. On the Hermeling
workshop, see Cologne 1980, pp. 89-132.
9. See Cologne 1981, p. 76, no. 36.
10. See ibid., p. 176, no. 93.

PENDANT WITH STANDING COUPLE
Vienna, workshop of Salomon Weininger, mid-19th century
Ronde-bosse enamel on gold, gold wire, and semi-precious stones
H: 52 mm. (2⅛ in.) W: 42 mm. (1⅝ in.) D: 17 mm. (¼ in.)
48.262   1948 *Purchase Fund*

PROVENANCE: Frederic Spitzer, Paris (sale, Anderson Galleries, New York, January 12, 1929, no. 609); Rosenau, Inc., New York; Joseph Brummer, New York

BIBLIOGRAPHY: Evans 1953, p. 63 n. 7

EXHIBITIONS: New York 1975, no. 248, p. 253; Ann Arbor 1975, no. 85, pp. 118-119, pl. 8

In 1876, it was discovered that a Viennese gold-smith, Salomon Weininger, entrusted some years earlier with the restoration of damaged objects in the Austrian Imperial Treasury in Vienna, had made copies of some of these pieces. He returned the forgeries in place of the originals and then sold the originals, and sometimes a second copy as well, to various private collectors.[1] Recently, the present enamel and a similar one in the Victoria and Albert Museum in London[2] (fig. 24) have been attributed to Weininger;[3] the latter differs only in that it lacks the gems and the gold fence around the garden. Showing a stylishly dressed couple, they duplicate a Netherlandish brooch of about 1430-1440 in the Imperial Treasury (fig. 25).[4]

Several features of the Boston and London enamels indicate that they are modern copies. In contrast to the differentiated faces on the original that show puffy cheeks and noses typical of the fifteenth century, the copies have similar faces for both male and female with a daintiness typical of the nineteenth century.[5] Furthermore, on the original the male figure wears a close-fitting cap with an upright trefoil brim below which his curly hair of coiled wire emerges. This medieval headdress seems not to have been understood by the copyist, who gave the male a gold crown and omitted the coiled locks in favor of a more cursory treatment of the hair. Similarly misunderstood are the three gold leaves over the figures' heads that, on the original, are branches emanating from a broken tree trunk in the center. On the Boston enamel three leaves, thinner and less intricately modeled than those on the original, emerge illogically from the twisted wire forming the fence; a simple rod supporting the two gems (in modern settings) has been substituted for the tree. The Boston copyist also misunderstood the function of the gold bars at the bottom of the fence that are arranged on the Vienna piece to indicate a gate; instead, he placed the bars in a random design. The enamel on the two copies is smoother than that on the original, and their blue, white, and green enamels contain large amounts of cobalt, lead, and chromium,[6] respectively, a factor that would be unusual in medieval work. Finally, the enamels contain neither tin nor antimony, commonly used as opacifiers in the middle ages.[7]

1. On Weininger, see Hayward 1974, pp. 170-179; Kurz 1948, 218-219.

2. Acc. no. M42-1975. (Formerly in the collection of Joan Evans, London.) See Evans 1953, p. 65.

3. Eikelmann 1984, p. 460. The dissertation provides an excellent comprehensive study of medieval *ronde-bosse* enamel.

4. Acc. no. PS 150, on exhibition in the Kunsthistorisches Museum in Vienna. See Eikelmann 1984, pp. 455-460; Müller and Steingräber 1954, p. 54, no. 37.

5. This observation was made by Renate Eikelmann.

6. On chromium and cobalt see p. xxi.

7. The enamel of the London piece was analyzed in 1975. On opacifiers see pp. xxi and xxii.

Fig. 24. Brooch with Standing Couple.
Imperial Treasury, Kunsthistorisches Museum, Vienna.

Fig. 25. Brooch with Standing Couple.
Victoria and Albert Museum, London.

Six plaques with Standing Saints:
James Major, a Female Martyr, John
the Baptist, Margaret, a Bishop, and
Dominic
Germany(?), 19th century
Champlevé enamel on silver
H: 70 mm. (2¾ in.) W: 26 mm. (1 in.) each
52.1533-1538   *John H. and Ernestine A. Payne Fund*

PROVENANCE: Wilhelm Clemens, Cologne; Paul
Wallraf, London

The facial types, the lack of volume in the drapery, and the precision with which the figures are
drawn all suggest that the enamels were made in
the nineteenth century. This hypothesis is supported by a neo-Gothic reliquary (fig. 26) from
the collection of Friedrich Culemann of Hanover
(1811-1884)[1] on which six virtually identical
plaques are placed around the body within
Gothic-style frames. Traces of solder on the backs
of the present plaques suggest that they too may
have been mounted on a similar object.

Analysis of the enamel and silver confirms
their modern manufacture. The silver has been
rolled and not hammered as it would have been
in the middle ages, and both the silver and the
cobalt blue enamel (filling the grounds and
engraved lines) come from different batches.[2]
While a medieval goldsmith is unlikely to have
had access to two sources of silver and cobalt, a
modern craftsman could easily purchase two different sheets of silver and two different batches
of commercially produced enamel powder.

1. Now in the Kestner Museum, Hanover (acc. no.
Z54).

2. Four plaques are made from silver with about 3.8
percent copper, and two have silver with about 4.6
percent copper. In the cobalt of the enamel on two
plaques there are sizable amounts of manganese, while
on the other four (including plaques made from both
groups of silver) manganese is not detectable.

Fig. 26. Reliquary with Enamel Plaques.
Kestner Museum, Hanover.

PLAQUE WITH CRUCIFIXION FLANKED BY
THE VIRGIN AND SAINT JOHN AND PER-
SONIFICATIONS OF CHURCH AND
SYNAGOGUE
Western Europe, 1904 – mid 1950s
Champlevé enamel and gilding on copper
H: 98 mm. (3⅞ in.) W: 166 mm. (6%16 in.)
59.518   *Edwin E. Jack Fund*
PROVENANCE: Galerie Fischer, Lucerne[1]

The design of the present plaque is nearly identical to that of one forming the top of a Lower
Saxon portable altar of the late twelfth century
(fig. 27) in the Victoria and Albert Museum in
London.[2] While the two differ in size and color,[3]
the dimensions of the Boston example corre-
spond exactly to those of a black-and-white photograph of the London plaque published in
1904,[4] suggesting that the photograph served as
its model.

Indeed, several misunderstandings or omis-
sions on the plaque may be explained by the
blurriness of the photograph in certain areas. For
example, the Virgin's ornamented wimple,
obscure in the photograph, has been misread by
the forger as curls on the top of the head, and
both the ornaments of Ecclesia's crown and the
toes of John's left foot, barely visible in the photograph, have been eliminated in the copy.

In general, the modeling lines on the Boston
plaque are sketchy and imprecise and lack the
sureness of their counterparts on the London
plaque. Furthermore, the combination of clear
enamel over the green of the cross and the blue
of the background is undocumented in examples
of the twelfth and thirteenth centuries. Radiographs reveal two unexplainable features of the
plaque: the copper is unusually porous, suggesting that it was cast; and two separate batches
of blue enamel were used in the ground. Also,
chromium has been detected in the green enamel
used on the border.[5]

1. According to the dealer, the piece came from a
private collection in Basel.

2. Acc. no. 4524-1858. See von Falke and Frauberger
1904, pp. 111-113.

3. The London piece, which is 3 mm. higher and 6
mm. wider than its counterpart in Boston, has gray,
blue, and white enamel (matching that on the plaques
forming the sides of the altar), while on the Boston
plaque blue, green, red, turquoise, and white enamel
are used.

4. See von Falke and Frauberger 1904, fig. 46.

5. For the significance of this element see p. xxi.

Fig. 27. Top of Portable Altar with Crucifixion.
Victoria and Albert Museum, London.

PART OF A CLASP
Western Europe, mid-19th – 20th century
Gilding on bronze and silver, *champlevé* enamel
and gilding on copper, and rock crystal
H: 137 mm. (5⅜ in.) W: 92 mm. (3⅝ in.)
49.490   *William Francis Warden Fund*

PROVENANCE: Durlacher Brothers, London and
New York; Joseph Brummer, New York (sale, Parke-
Bernet, May 14, 1949, no. 716)

BIBLIOGRAPHY: *Boston Museum Bulletin* 1957, p. 76,
no. 24

EXHIBITIONS: Boston 1940, no. 217

The object is unique; the wide loop suggests that
it formed one side of a clasp,[1] but the presence of
a crystal on such an object, as well as its placement over an enamel, is unprecedented and unexplainable. Such crystals usually magnify relics.
Other condemning features are the painted red-
dot design on the sides, the use of gilt-silver
filigree on a bronze base, and the design of the
filigree – double-stranded *rinceaux* with tiny pine
cones. All are without parallel on medieval
objects. Although in palette and design the
enamels are reminiscent of those on the phylac-
tery of Marie of Oignies in Brussels[2] (which may
have served as their model), the presence of uranium and chromium in the green[3] and the partic-
ulate nature of all the enamels suggest that they
are modern.

1. A thirteenth-century Limoges enamel of similar
shape but without the crystal, whose use has not been
determined, is preserved in Lille (Musée des Beaux-
Arts acc. no. 56).

2. Musée Cinquantenaire acc. no. 3673; made in
Namur and datable about 1230. See Collon-Gevaert
1972, pp. 290-291.

3. See pp. xxi and xxii.

Ainaud de Lasarte 1973
Ainaud de Lasarte, Joan. *Art Romànic Guia*. Barcelona, 1973.

Alexander 1978
Alexander, Jonathan J. G. *Insular Manuscripts, 6th to the 9th Century*. London, 1978.

Andersson 1976
Andersson, Britt-Marie. "Les Trésors d'émaux limousins en Suède Médiévale," *Bulletin de la Societé archéologique et historique du Limousin* 103 (1976), pp. 107-136.

Andersson 1980
Andersson, Britt-Marie. "Emaux limousins en Suède, les châsses, les croix," *Kungl. Vitterhets Historie och Antikvitets Akademien, Antikvariskat Arkiv.* 69 (1980), pp. 1-91.

Ann Arbor 1975
Levin, William; Olds, Clifton; and Williams, Ralph. *Images of Love and Death in Late Medieval and Renaissance Art*. University of Michigan Museum of Art, Ann Arbor, 1975-1976.

Apollo 1925
"Some Early Enamels in the Collection of Lord Carmichael," *Apollo* 2 (1925), pp. 128-132.

Armstrong 1922
Armstrong, E. C. R. "Lord Emly's Shrine; Two Ridge-Poles of Shrines, and Two Bronze Castings." *Antiquaries Journal* 2 (1922), pp. 135-137.

Arras 1935
Exposition de Notre-Dame des Ardents et du Calvaire d'Arras dans l'art et le folklore. Arras, 1935.

Avril 1978
Avril, François. *Manuscript Painting at the Court of France* (1310-1380). New York, 1978.

Avril et al. 1983
Avril, François; Barral i Altet, Xavier; and Gaborit-Chopin, Danielle. *Les Royaumes d'occident*. Paris, 1983.

Barbier de Montault 1898
Barbier de Montault, Xavier. "Un Crucifix habillé du XIIIᵉ siècle," *Bulletin de la Société scientifique, historique, et archéologique de la Corrèze* 20 (1898), pp. 573-583.

Baxandall 1980
Baxandall, Michael. *The Limewood Sculptors of Renaissance Germany*. New Haven, 1980.

Bertelli 1969
Bertelli, Carlo. "Traversie della tomba di Clemente IV," *Paragone* 227 (1969), pp. 53-63.

Bertelli 1970
Bertelli, Carlo. "Vetri italiani a fondo d'oro del secolo XIII," *Journal of Glass Studies* 12 (1970), pp. 70-78.

Bertelli 1973a
Bertelli, Carlo. "La mitra di San Ranieri: altri vetri-dorati dell'Italia meridionale," *Paragone* 275 (1973), pp. 64-71.

Bertelli 1973b
Bertelli, Carlo. "Vetri a oro del Trecento padano," *Paragone* 275 (1973), pp. 71-81.

Bilimoff 1978
Bilimoff, Michèle. "Pyxides d'origine limousine conservées en France." Master's thesis, University of Paris, 1978.

Birmingham 1936
Catalogue of an Heraldic Exhibition. City Museum and Art Gallery, Birmingham (U.K.), 1936.

Blair and Campbell 1983
Blair, Claude, and Campbell, Marian. "Le Mystère de Monsieur Marcy," *Connaissance des Arts* 375 (1983), pp. 70-73.

Bossert 1932
Bossert, H. Th. *Geschichte des Kunstgewerbes aller Zeiten und Völker*. Vol. 5. Berlin, 1932.

Boston 1940
Arts of the Middle Ages 1000-1400. Museum of Fine Arts, Boston, 1940.

Boston 1981
Masterpieces from the Boston Museum. Museum of Fine Arts, Boston, 1981.

Boston Museum Annual Report 1968
The Museum Year, 1968 (Museum of Fine Arts Annual Report). Boston, 1968.

Boston Museum Bulletin 1957
Bulletin of the Museum of Fine Arts, Boston 50 (1957) pp. 53-119.

Botkine 1911
Collection M. P. Botkine. St. Petersburg, 1911.

Branner 1977
Branner, Robert. *Manuscript Painting in Paris during the Reign of Saint Louis*. Berkeley, 1977.

Brault 1973
Brault, Gérard. *Eight Thirteenth-Century Rolls of Arms in French and Anglo-Norman Blazon*. University Park, 1973.

Braun 1940
Braun, J. *Die Reliquiare, des Christlichen Kultes und Ihre Entwicklung*. Freiburg im Breisgau, 1940.

British Museum 1924
British Museum: A Guide to the Mediaeval Antiquities and Objects of Later Date. London, 1924.

Brodsky 1972
Brodsky, Joyce. "The Stavelot Triptych:Notes on a Mosan Work." *Gesta* 11 (1972), pp. 19-33.

Brown 1984
Brown, Katharine. *Frankish Art in American Collections*. New York, 1984.

Bruges 1960
Le Siècle des primitifs flamands. Musée Communal des Beaux-Arts, Bruges, 1960.

Buckton 1981
Buckton, David. "The Mass-Produced Byzantine Saint," *Studios Supplementary to Sobornost* 5 (1981), pp. 187-188.

Burty 1869
Burty, Philippe. *Chefs-d'oeuvre des arts industriels*. Paris, 1869.

Buschhausen 1980
Buschhausen, Helmut. *Der Verduner Altar*. Vienna, 1980.

Cahn 1967
Cahn, Walter. *The Souvigny Bible: A Study in Romanesque Manuscript Illumination*. Ph.D. dissertation, New York University, 1967.

Cambridge 1975
Eucharistic Vessels of the Middle Ages. Busch-Reisinger Museum, Cambridge (Mass.), 1975.

Cambridge 1978
Caviness, Madeline. *Medieval and Renaissance Stained Glass from New England Collections*. Busch-Reisinger Museum, Cambridge, 1978.

Campbell 1979
Campbell, Marian. "Scribe faber lima," *Burlington Magazine* 121 (1979), pp. 364-369.

Campbell 1980
Campbell, Marian. "The Campion Hall Triptych and its Workshop," *Apollo* 110, pp. 418-423.

Campbell 1983
Campbell, Marian. *Medieval Enamels*. London, 1983.

Cassebaum 1983
Cassebaum, Heinz. "Neue Aspekte zur Entdeckung des tzens von Glas," *Silikattechnik* 34 (1983), pp. 213-214.

Caudron 1976
Caudron, Simone. "Emaux champlevés de Limoges et amateurs britanniques du XVIIIᵉ siècle," *Bulletin de la Société archéologique et historique du Limousin* 103 (1976), pp. 137-168.

Caviness 1970
Caviness, Madeline H. "Fifteenth Century Stained Glass from the Chapel of Hampton Court, Herefordshire: The Apostles' Creed and Other Subjects," *Walpole Society Publications* 42 (1970), pp. 35-60.

Caviness 1985
Caviness, Madeline H., ed. "Stained Glass before 1700 in American Collections New England and New York (*Corpus Vitrearum*, Checklist I)," *Studies in the History of Art* vol. 15. Washington, D.C., 1985.

Charleston 1980
Charleston, Robert. "Acid-Etching on Glass," *Glass Circle* 2 (1980), pp. 31-39.

Chicago 1970
Rowe, Donald. *Enamels of the XIIth to the XVIth Century*. Martin d'Arcy Gallery of Art, Chicago, 1970.

Cleveland 1967
Wixom, William. *Treasures from Medieval France*. Cleveland Museum of Art, 1967.

Collon-Gevaert 1951
Collon-Gevaert, S. *Histoire des arts du métal en Belgique*. Brussels, 1951.

Collon-Gevaert 1972
Collon-Gevaert, Suzanne; Lejeune, Jean; and Stiennon, Jacques. *A Treasury of Romanesque Art*. Brussels, 1972.

Cologne 1964a
Degen, Kurt, et al. *Die Sammlungen des Baron von Hüpsch Ein Kölner Kunst Kabinett um 1800*. Schnütgen-Museum, Cologne, 1964.

Cologne 1964b
Schnitzler, Hermann. *Der Meister des Dreikönigen-Schreins*. Cologne, 1964.

Cologne 1975
Monumenta Annonis. Schnütgen-Museum, Cologne, 1975.

Cologne 1980
Goldschmiedearbeiten des Historismus in Köln. Kolnisches Stadtmuseum, Cologne, 1980.

Cologne 1981
Email: Kunst, Handwerk, Industrie. Kölnisches Stadtmuseum, Cologne, 1981.

Cologne 1985
Ornamenta Ecclesia Kunst und Kunstler der Romanik in Köln. 3 vols. (Anton Legner, ed.) Cologne, 1985.

Cornforth 1973
Cornforth, John. "Hampton Court, Herefordshire – III," *Country Life* (March 8, 1973), p. 584.

Crawford 1923
Crawford, Henry S. "A Descriptive List of Irish Shrines and Reliquaries," *Journal of the Royal Society of Antiquaries of Ireland* 53 (1923), pp. 74-93; 151-176.

Dalton 1912
Dalton, O.M. *Fitzwilliam Museum McClean Bequest.* Cambridge, 1912.

Darcel 1865
Darcel, Alfred. "Union centrale des beaux arts appliqués à l'industrie. Musée Rétrospectif. Le Moyen Age," *Gazette des Beaux-Arts* 19 (1865), pp. 289-303, 427-445, 507-533.

Darcel 1891
Darcel, Alfred. *Notice des émaux et de l'orfèvrerie.* Paris, 1891.

Degen 1955
Degen, K. *Frühmittelalterliches Kunsthandwerk.* Darmstadt, 1955.

Detroit 1960
Flanders in the Fifteenth Century: Art and Civilization. Detroit Institute of Arts, 1960.

Detroit Bulletin 1951
"Recent Acquisitions of Ancient and Medieval Art," *Detroit Institute of Arts Bulletin* 31 (1951), pp. 59-80.

Dijon 1962
La Sainte-Chapelle de Dijon, Siège de l'Ordre de la Toison d'Or. Musée de Dijon, Palais des Ducs de Bourgogne, 1962.

Dingley 1867
Dingley, Thomas. *History from Marble.* London, 1867.

Dinkler-von Schubert 1964
Dinkler-von Schubert, E. *Der Schrein der Hl. Elisabeth zu Marburg.* Marburg-sur-la-Lahn, 1964.

Dodwell 1961
Theophilus. *Diversarum artium schedula* (C. R. Dodwell, ed.). London, 1961.

Durliat 1956
Durliat, Marcel. *Christs romans du Roussillon et de Cerdagne.* Perpignan, 1956.

Eikelmann 1984
Eikelmann, Renate. *Franko-Flämische Emailplastik des Spätmittelalters.* Ph.D. dissertation, Ludwig-Maximilians University, Munich, 1984.

Encyclopédie 1870
L'Art pour tous. Encyclopédie de l'art industriel et décoratif. Vol. 248. Paris, 1870.

Von Euw and Plotzek 1979
Von Euw, Anton, and Plotzek, Joachim. *Die Handschriften der Sammlung Ludwig.* Cologne, 1979.

Evans 1953
Evans, Joan. *A History of Jewellery 1100-1870.* London, 1953.

Von Falke and Frauberger 1904
Von Falke, Otto, and Frauberger, Heinrich. *Deutsche Schmelzarbeiten des Mittelalters.* Frankfurt, 1904.

Von Falke 1929
Von Falke, Otto. "Die Schmucksammlung Marc Rosenberg," *Pantheon* 3 (1929), pp. 416-417.

Flinn 1963
Flinn, John. *Le Roman de Renart.* Toronto, 1963.

Forrer 1893
Forrer, Robert. *Die frühchristlichen Alterthümer aus dem Gräberfelde von Achmim-Panopolis.* Strasbourg, 1893.

François 1981
François, Geneviève. "Croix aragonaises émaillées au xive siècle," *Actes du 104e Congrès national des Sociétés Savantes, Bordeaux 1979.* Bordeaux, 1981, pp. 317-334.

Frankfurt 1966
Katalog Kunst und Kunsthandwerk. Museum für Kunsthandwerk, Frankfurt, 1966.

Frankfurt 1982
Europäische Emailkunst von 1150-1900. Museum für Kunsthandwerk, Frankfurt, 1982.

Freeman 1963
Freeman, Margaret. "A Shrine for a Queen," *Metropolitan Museum of Art Bulletin* 21 (1963), pp. 327-339.

Fritz 1982
Fritz, Johann Michael. *Goldschmiedekunst der Gotik in Mitteleuropa.* Munich, 1982.

Gaborit 1976
Gaborit, Jean-René. "L'Autel majeur de Grandmont," *Cahiers de civilisation médiévale* 19 (1976), pp. 231-246.

Gaborit-Chopin 1969
Gaborit-Chopin, Danielle. *La Décoration des manuscrits à Saint-Martial de Limoges et en Limousin du IXᵉ au XIIᵉ siècle*. Paris and Geneva, 1969.

Garnier 1886
Garnier, Edouard. *Histoire de la verrerie et de l'émaillerie*. Tours, 1886.

Gauthier 1950
Gauthier, Marie-Madeleine. *Emaux limousins champlevés des XIIᵉ, XIIIᵉ et XIVᵉ siècles*. Paris, 1950.

Gauthier 1964
Gauthier, Marie-Madeleine. "Le Gout Plantagenet," *Internationalen Kongresses für Kunstgeschichte* 21 (1964), pp. 139-155.

Gauthier 1966
Gauthier, Marie-Madeleine. "Observations chronologiques sur les émaux champlevés méridionaux et limousins exposés parmi les trésors des églises de France." *Les monuments historiques de la France* 12 (1966), pp. 81-91.

Gauthier 1967
Gauthier, Marie-Madeleine. "L'Ange 'grand comme nature,' jadis pivotant au sommet de la flêche de Saint-Pierre du Dorat." *Bulletin de la Société archéologique et historique du Limousin* 94 (1967), pp. 109-129.

Gauthier 1968
Gauthier, Marie-Madeleine. "Les Collections d'émaux champlevés acquisitions récentes." *Revue du Louvre* 6 (1968), pp. 447-454.

Gauthier 1972
Gauthier, Marie-Madeleine. *Emaux du moyen âge occidental*. Paris, 1972.

Gauthier 1973
Gauthier, Marie-Madeleine. "Une Colombe limousine prise aux rets d'un 'antiquaire' Benedictin à Saint-Germain-des-Près," *Intuition und Kunstwissenschaft. Festschrift für Hanns Swarzenski*. Berlin, 1973, pp. 171-190.

Gauthier 1978a
Gauthier, Marie-Madeleine. "Du tabernacle au retable: Une innovation limousine vers 1230," *Revue de l'art* 40-41 (1978), pp. 23-42.

Gauthier 1978b
Gauthier, Marie-Madeleine. "La Croix émaillée de Bonneval au musée de Cluny," *Revue du Louvre* 4 (1978), pp. 267-285.

Gauthier 1979
Gauthier, Marie-Madeleine. "Emaux septentrionaux, colloque du British Museum, 17-18-19 novembre, 1978," *Revue de l'art* 43 (1979), pp. 79-82.

Gauthier 1981
Gauthier, Marie-Madeleine. "Un Style et ses lieux: les ornements métalliques de la Bible de Souvigny," *Gesta* 20 (1981), pp. 141-153.

Gauthier and François 1981
Gauthier, Marie-Madeleine, and François, Geneviève. *Medieval Enamels, Masterpieces from the Keir Collection*. London, 1981.

Gauthier 1985
Gauthier, Marie-Madeleine. *Catalogue international de l'oeuvre de Limoges*. Vol. 1: *L'Europe romane 1100-1190, innovations méridionales*. Paris, 1985.

Gay 1887
Gay, Victor. *Glossaire archéologique du Moyen Age et de la Renaissance*. 2 vols. Paris, 1887-1928.

Giraud 1881
Giraud, Jean-Baptiste. *Les Arts du métal. Recueil déscriptif et raisonné des principaux objets ayant figuré à l'exposition de 1880*. Paris, 1881.

Gordon 1965
Gordon, James. "The Articles of the Creed and the Apostles," *Speculum* 40 (1965), pp. 634-640.

Green 1961
Green, Rosalie. "Ex Ungue Leonem," *De Artibus Opscula XL: Essays in Honor of Erwin Panofsky*. New York, 1961, pp. 157-169.

Guth-Dreyfus 1954
Guth-Dreyfus, Katia. *Basler Studien zur Kunstgeschichte*. Vol. 9: *Translucides Email in der ersten Halfte des 14 Jahrhunderts am Ober, Mittel-und Niederrhein*. Basel, 1954.

Hahnloser 1971
Hahnloser, H.R. *Il Tesoro di San Marco*. Florence, 1971.

Halm and Berliner 1931
Halm, P.M., and Berliner, R. *Das Hallesche Heiltum*. Berlin, 1931.

Hamburg 1961
Sechs Sammlerstellen aus Museum für Kunst und Gewerbe. Hamburg, 1961.

Hartford 1967
Bulletin of the Wadsworth Atheneum, Hartford, 1967.

Hausherr 1962
Hausherr, Reiner. "Das Imerwardkreuz und der Volto-Santo-Typ," *Zeitschrift für Kunstwissenschaft* 14 (1962), pp. 129-170.

Havard 1896
Havard, Henry. *Histoire de l'orfèvrerie française*. Paris, 1896.

Hawes 1928
Hawes, Charles. "A Medallion of Byzantine Cloisonné Enamel," *Bulletin* of the Museum of Fine Arts 26 (1928), pp. 56-57.

Hayward 1974
Hayward, J. F. "Salomon Weininger, Master Faker," *Connoisseur* 187 (1974), pp. 170-179.

Henry 1956
Henry, Françoise. "Irish Enamels of the Dark Ages and their Relation to the Cloisonné Techniques," *Dark Age Britain, Studies Presented to E. T. Leeds* (D. B. Harden, ed.) London, 1956.

Heuser 1959
Heuser, Hans-Jörgen. "Ein Profangefäss um 1300," *Wallraf-Richartz-Jahrbuch* 21 (1959), pp. 215-220.

Heuser 1974
Heuser, Hans-Jörgen. *Oberrhenische Goldschmiedekunst im Hochmittelalter*. Berlin, 1974.

Horat 1982
Horat, Heinz. "Ein Bursenreliquiar aus dem Entlebuch," *Zeitschrift für Schweizerische Archäologie und Kunstgeschichte* 39 (1982), pp. 58-75.

Horstman 1901
Horstman, Carl. *Nova Legenda Anglie*. Oxford 1901.

Huber 1969
Huber, P. *Athos: Leben, Glaube, Kunst*. Zurich, 1969.

Hunter 1958
Hunter, Sam. "A Plaque from Limoges," *Minneapolis Institute of Arts Bulletin* 47 (1958), pp. 28-33.

Jansen 1964
Jansen, Ad. *Art chrétien jusqu'à la fin du moyen âge*. Brussels, 1964.

Joffroy 1974
Joffroy, René. *Le Cimetière de Lavoye nécropole mérovingienne*. Paris, 1974.

Karnaghan 1928
Karnaghan, Anne Webb. "The New Wing for Decorative Arts of Europe and America," *Bulletin* of the Museum of Fine Arts, Boston 26 (1928), pp. 96-110.

Kauffmann 1975
Kauffmann, C. M. *Romanesque Manuscripts* 1066-1190. London, 1975.

Kesseler 1951
Kesseler, C. "Die Wiederherstellung des Albinusschreines," *Rheinische Kirchen im Wiederaufbau* (1951), pp. 41-45.

Koechlin 1924
Koechlin, Raymond. *Les Ivoires gothiques français*. Paris, 1924.

Kötzsche 1973a
Kötzsche, Dietrich. "Zum Stand der Forschung der Goldschmiedekunst des 12 Jahrhunderts im Rhein-Maas-Gebiet," *Rhein und Maas Kunst und Kultur 800-1400*. Cologne, 1973, pp. 191-236.

Kötzsche 1973b
Kötzsche, Dietrich. *Der Welfenschatz im Berliner Kunstgewerbemuseum*. Berlin, 1973.

Kohlhaussen 1931
Kohlhaussen, Heinrich. "Niederlandisch Schmelzwerk," *Jahrbuch der Preuszischen Kunstsammlungen* 52 (1931), pp. 153-169.

Kovacs 1968
Kovacs, Eva. *L'Oeuvre de Limoges en Hongrie*. Budapest, 1968.

Kurz 1948
Kurz, Otto. *Fakes: A Handbook for Collectors and Students*. New Haven, 1948.

Labarte 1847
Labarte, Jules. *Description des objets d'art qui composent la collection Debruge-Dumenil*. Paris, 1847.

de Laborde 1853
de Laborde, Léon. *Notice des émaux, bijoux et objets divers exposés dans les galeries du Musée du Louvre*. Paris, 1853.

Lafontaine-Dosogne 1975
Lafontaine-Dosogne, J. "Oeuvres d'art mosan au Musée de l'Hermitage à Leningrad," *Revue Belge d'archéologie et d'histoire de l'art* 44 (1975), pp. 85-107.

Lapkovskaya 1971
Lapkovskaya, E. A. *Applied Art of the Middle Ages in the Collection of the State Hermitage*. Leningrad, 1971.

Lasko 1972
Lasko, Peter. *Ars Sacra 800-1400*. Harmondsworth, 1972.

Le Goff 1964
Le Goff, Jacques. *La Civilisation de l'occident médiéval*. Paris, 1964.

Lexikon 1968-1976
Lexikon der Christlichen Ikonographie. 8 vols. Freiburg, 1968-1976.

Liège 1905
Exposition universelle et internationale de Liège. Exposition de l'art ancien au pays de Liège. Catalogue général. Liège, 1905.

Liège 1930
Exposition internationale de Liège. Exposition de l'art de l'ancien pays de Liège et des anciens arts Wallons. Liège, 1930.

Liège 1951
Art mosan et arts anciens du pays de Liège. Liège, 1951.

Liège 1980
Lemeunier, A., and Pirenne-Hulin, F. *Oeuvres maîtresses du musée d'art religieux et d'art Mosan.* Basilique Saint-Martin, Liège, 1980.

Lightbown 1978
Lightbown, R.W. *Secular Goldsmiths' Work in Medieval France: A History.* London, 1978.

Limoges 1948
Emaux limousins, xii^c, xiii^c, xiv^c siècles. Limoges, 1948.

Limoges 1977
Collection Egyptienne, Emaux: Guide du Musée Municipal. Limoges, 1977.

De Linas 1881
De Linas, Charles. *Emaillerie, métallurgie. Expositions rétrospectives en 1880, Bruxelles, Düsseldorf.* Paris, 1881, p. 189f.

London 1936
Gothic Art in Europe. Burlington Fine Arts Club. London, 1936.

London 1979
The Golden Age of Venetian Glass. British Museum, London, 1979.

London 1984
English Romanesque Art 1066-1200. Hayward Gallery, London, 1984.

Mahr 1941
Mahr, A. *Christian Art in Ancient Ireland.* Vol. 2 (J. Raftery, ed.) Dublin, 1941.

Mallé 1950
Mallé, L. "Antichismalti cloisonnés e champlevés dei sec 11-13 in raccolte e musei del Piemonte," *Societa Piemontese di archeologia e belli arti, Bollettino* 4-5 (1950-1951), pp. 80-122.

Mancinelli 1973
Mancinelli, Fabrizio. "Reliquie e Reliquiari ad Abbadia S. Salvatore," *Pontifica Academia Romana di Archeologia Rendiconti* 46 (1973-1974), pp. 251-71.

Marks and Morgan 1981
Marks, Richard, and Morgan, Nigel. *The Golden Age of English Manuscript Painting 1200-1500.* New York, 1981.

Marquet de Vasselot 1906
Marquet de Vasselot, J. J. *Catalogue raisonné de la Collection Martin le Roy, 1, Orfèvrerie et émaillerie.* Paris, 1906.

Marquet de Vasselot 1941
Marquet de Vasselot, J. J. *Les Crosses limousines du xiii^c siècle.* Paris, 1941.

Marstrander 1963
Marstrander, Sverre. "A Norwegian Find from the Viking Period with Western European Imported Goods; Irish Reliquary and Hanging Bowl Found in Romsdal," *Lochlann* 3 (1963), pp. 1-36.

Maurer 1954
Maurer, Emil. *Die Kunstdenkmäler des Kantons Aargau, III, Das Kloster Königsfelden. Kunstdenkmäler der Schweiz.* Vol. 32. Basel, 1954.

Meiss 1974
Meiss, Millard. *French Painting in the Time of Jean de Berry, The Limbourgs and their Contemporaries.* New York, 1974.

Merrifield 1849
Merrifield, M. P. *Original Treatises, Dating from the XIIth to the XVIIIth Centuries on the Arts of Painting.* 2 vols. London, 1849.

Mezey 1979
Mezey, Nicole. "Creed and Prophets Series in the Visual Arts, with a note on examples in York," *Edam Newsletter* 2 (1979), pp. 7-10.

Millar 1959
Millar, Eric. *The Parisian Miniaturist Honoré.* London, 1959.

Milliken 1927
Milliken, W. "A Reliquary of Champlevé Enamel from the Valley of the Meuse. The J.H. Wade Collection," *Bulletin* of the Cleveland Museum of Art 14 (1927), pp. 51-54.

Molinier 1888
Molinier, Emile. *Inventaire du trésor du St. Siège sous Boniface VIII* (Extrait de la Bibliothèque de l'Ecole des Chartes). Paris, 1888.

Molinier 1900
Molinier, Emile. *Histoire général des arts appliqués à l'industrie.* Vol. 4: *L'Orfèvrerie religieuse et civile.* Paris, 1900.

Molinier 1903
Molinier, Emile. *Collections du château de Goluchow.* Paris, 1903.

Morgan 1973
Morgan, Nigel. "The Iconography of the Twelfth-Century Mosan Enamels," *Rhein und Maas.* Vol. 2. Cologne, 1973, pp. 263-278.

Mowinckel 1925
Mowinckel, Rolf. "Hundorpskrinet," *De Sandvigske Samlinger, Arsberetning 1923-1924.* Oslo, 1925, pp. 5-23.

Müller and Steingräber 1954
Müller, Theodor, and Steingräber, Erich. "Die Französische Goldemailplastik um 1400," *Münchener Jahrbuch der Bildenden Kunst* 5 (1954), pp. 29-79.

Mütherich 1941
Mütherich, Florentine. *Die Ornamentik der rheinischen Goldschmiedekunst in der Stauferzeit.* Würzburg, 1941.

Muñoz 1911
Muñoz, A. *Pièces de choix de la collection du Comte Grégoire Stroganoff à Rome.* Vol. 2. Rome, 1911.

Murphy 1892
Murphy, Denis. "The Shrine of Saint Callin of Fenagh," *Journal of the Royal Society of Antiquaries of Ireland* 22 (1892), pp. 151-153.

New York 1968
Gomez-Moreno, Carmen. *Medieval Art from Private Collections.* Metropolitan Museum of Art, New York, 1968.

New York 1970
The Year 1200. Metropolitan Museum of Art, New York, 1970.

New York 1975
The Secular Spirit: Life and Art at the End of the Middle Ages. Metropolitan Museum of Art, New York, 1975.

New York 1977
Treasures of Irish Art 1500 B.C.-1500 A.D. Metropolitan Museum of Art, New York, 1977.

New York 1983
Notable Acquisitions 1982-1983. Metropolitan Museum of Art, New York, 1983.

Oman 1967
Oman, C. C. "The Whithorn Crozier, a Newly Discovered English Enamel," *Burlington Magazine* 109 (1967), pp. 299-300.

Ostoia 1959
Ostoia, Vera K. "The Lusignan Mirror." *Metropolitan Museum Bulletin* 18 (1959), pp. 18-27.

Otavsky 1973
Otavsky, Karel. "Zu einer Gruppe von Kupferreliefs aus dem 13. Jahrhundert," *Artes minores. Dank an Werner Abegg.* Riggisberg, 1973, pp. 37-74.

Ottawa 1972
Brieger, Peter, and Verdier, Philippe. *Art and the Courts.* National Gallery of Canada, Ottawa, 1972.

Paris 1957
Chefs-d'oeuvres romans des musées de Province. Musée du Louvre, Paris, 1957.

Paris 1965
Les Trésors des églises de France. Musée des Arts Décoratifs, Paris, 1965.

Paris 1968
L'Europe gothique. Musée du Louvre, Paris, 1968.

Paris 1981a
Les Fastes du Gothique, le siècle de Charles V. Galeries Nationales du Grand Palais, Paris, 1981.

Paris 1981b
Jean Fouquet. Musée du Louvre, Paris, 1981.

Peraté 1911
Peraté, A. *Collection G. Hoentschel.* Vol. 2. Paris, 1911.

Perls 1940
Perls, Klaus. *Jean Fouquet.* Paris, 1940.

Petersen 1907
Petersen, Th. "A Celtic Reliquary Found in a Norwegian Burial-Mound," *Det kongelige Norske Videnskabers Selskab Forhandlinger* 8 (1907), pp. 1-21.

Pottier and Willemin 1839
Pottier, André, and Willemin, N. X. *Monuments français inédits.* Paris, 1839.

Providence 1977
Transformations of the Court Style: Gothic Art in Europe, 1270 to 1330. Museum of Art, Rhode Island School of Design, Providence, 1977.

Reiners 1925
Reiners, Heribert. *Die Kölner Malerschule.* Mönchen-Gladbach, 1925.

Rickert 1952
Rickert, Margaret. *The Reconstructed Carmelite Missal.* Chicago, 1952.

Robinson 1873
Robinson, Charles G. *The Mansions and Manors of Herefordshire.* Hereford, 1873.

Rogers and Goetz 1945
Rogers, Meyric R., and Goetz, Oswald. *Handbook to the Lucy Maud Buckingham Medieval Collection*. Art Institute of Chicago, 1945.

Röhrig 1955
Röhrig, Floridus. *Der Verduner Altar*. Vienna, 1955.

Rosenberg 1911
Rosenberg, Marc. "Studien über Goldschmiedekunst in der Sammlung Figdor-Wien," *Kunst und Kunsthandwerk* 14 (1911) pp. 329-404.

Rosenberg 1918
Rosenberg, Marc. "Erster Zellenschmelz nordlich der Alpen," *Jahrbuch der Preuszischen Kunstsammlungen* 39 (1918), pp. 1-50.

Rosenberg 1922
Rosenberg, Marc. *Zellenschmelz III*. Darmstadt, 1922.

Rosenberg 1928
Der Goldschmiede Merkzeichen. 4 vols. Cologne, 1923-1928.

Ross 1939
Ross, Marvin. "An Enameled Reliquary from Champagnat," *Medieval Studies in Memory of A. Kingsley Porter*. Vol. 2. Cambridge, 1939, pp. 467-477.

Ross 1962
Ross, Marvin. *Catalogue of the Byzantine and Early Medieval Antiquities in the Dumbarton Oaks Collection*. Vol. 1: *Metalwork, Ceramics, Glass, Glyptics, Painting*. Washington, D.C., 1962.

Rossacher 1966
Rossacher, Kurt. *Der Schatz des Erzstiftes Salzburg*. Salzburg, 1966.

Rossi 1929
Rossi, F. "Un reliquario con vetri dorati del Museo Nazionale di Firenze," *Dedalo* 9 (1929), pp. 707-714.

Ruckert 1959
Ruckert, Rainer. "Beiträge zur limousiner Plastik des 13 Jahrhunderts," *Zeitschrift für Kunstgeschichte* 22 (1959), pp. 1-16.

Rupin 1890
Rupin, Ernst. *L'Oeuvre Limoges*. Paris, 1890.

San Francisco 1915
Colosanti, A. *Catalogue of the Canessa Collection* (Pacific International Exposition). San Francisco, 1915.

Sandoz 1959
Sandoz, Marc. *Catalogue d'art pre-roman et roman du Musée des Beaux-Arts*. Poitiers, 1959.

Schilling 1950
Schilling, Rosy. "Studien zur deutschen Goldschmiedekunst des 12 und 13 Jahrhunderts." *Form und Inhalt. Kunstgeschichtliche Studien Otto Schmitt zum 60 Geburtstag*. Stuttgart, 1950, pp. 73-88.

Schnitzler 1959
Schnitzler, Hermann. *Rheinische Schatzkammer Die Romanik*. Düsseldorf, 1959.

Schnitzler 1965
Schnitzler, Hermann; Bloch, Peter; and Ratton, Charles. *Email, Goldschmiede-und Metallarbeiten: Europäisches Mittelalter, Sammlung E. und M. Kofler-Truniger, Luzern*. Lucerne, 1965.

Scott 1982
Scott, Kathleen. "Lydgate's Lives of Saints Edmund and Fremund: A Newly Located Manuscript in Arundel Castle," *Viator* 13 (1982), pp. 335-366.

Siple 1928
Siple, Ella. "Byzantine Enamels in Detroit, Worcester and Boston," *Burlington Magazine* 53 (1928), pp. 197-198.

Skinner 1933
Skinner, Orin. "Stained Glass in the Boston Museum of Fine Arts," *Stained Glass*, 1933-1934.

Souchal 1963
Souchal, Geneviève. "Les Emaux de Grandmont au xiie siècle," *Bulletin Monumental* 121 (1963), pp. 123-150.

Sowers 1965
Sowers, Robert. *Stained Glass: An Architectural Art*. New York, 1965.

Steinberg 1983
Steinberg, Leo. *The Sexuality of Christ in Renaissance Art and in Modern Oblivion*. New York, 1983.

Steingräber 1963
Steingräber, Erich. "Venezianische Goldschmiedekunst des 15. Jahrhunderts," *Mitteilungen des Kunsthistorischen Institutes* 10 (1963), pp. 147-192.

Stettler and Otavsky 1973
Stettler, M., and Otavsky, K. *Abegg-Stiftung Bern in Riggisberg*. Berne, 1973.

Stohlman 1939
Stohlman, F. *Gli Smalti del Museo Sacro Vaticano*. Rome, 1939.

Stokstad 1983
Stokstad, Marilyn. *Medieval Enamels and Sculptures from the Keir Collection*. Kansas City, 1983.

Stratford 1984
Stratford, Neil. "Three English Romanesque Enamelled Ciboria," *Burlington Magazine* 126 (1984), pp. 204-216.

Stuttgart 1977
Die Zeit Der Staufer-Geschichte, Kunst, Kultur. Vols. 1-4. Württembergisches Landesmuseum, Stuttgart, 1977.

Stuttmann 1966
Stuttmann, Ferdinand. *Bildkataloge des Kestner-Museums, Hannover VIII: Mittelalter I, Bronze, Email, Elfenbein.* Hannover, 1966.

G. Swarzenski 1926a
Swarzenski, Georg. "Das Auftreten des Eglomisé bei Nicolo Pisano," *Festschrift Paul Clemen.* Düsseldorf, 1926, pp. 326ff.

G. Swarzenski 1926b
Swarzenski, Georg. "Venezianische Glasminiaturen des Mittelalters," *Städel-Jahrbuch* 5 (1926), pp. 13-16.

G. Swarzenski and Schilling 1929
Swarzenski, Georg; Schilling, Rosy. *Die Illuminierten Handschriften und Einzelminiaturen des Mittelalters und der Renaissance in Frankfurter Besitz.* Frankfurt, 1929.

G. Swarzenski 1932
Swarzenski, Georg. "Aus dem Kunstkreis Heinrichs des Löwen," *Städel-Jahrbuch* 7-8 (1932), pp. 241-395.

G. Swarzenski 1940
Swarzenski, Georg. "Localization of Medieval Verre Eglomisé in the Walters Collection," *Journal of the Walters Art Gallery* 3 (1940), pp. 55-68.

G. Swarzenski 1949
Swarzenski, Georg. "Profane Work in the High Middle Ages," *Bulletin* of the Museum of Fine Arts, Boston 47 (1949), pp. 71-81.

G. Swarzenski 1951
Swarzenski, Georg. "A Masterpiece of Limoges," *Bulletin* of the Museum of Fine Arts, Boston 49 (1951), pp. 17-25.

G. Swarzenski 1954
Swarzenski, Georg. "An Early Anglo-Irish Portable Shrine," *Bulletin* of the Museum of Fine Arts, Boston 52 (1954), pp. 50-62.

H. Swarzenski 1952
Swarzenski, Hanns. "An Unknown Carolingian Ivory," *Bulletin* of the Museum of Fine Arts, Boston 50 (1952), pp. 2-7.

H. Swarzenski 1953
Swarzenski, Hanns. "The Italian and Mosan Shows in the Light of the Great Art Exhibitions," *Burlington Magazine* 95 (1953), pp. 152-157.

H. Swarzenski 1954
Swarzenski, Hanns. *Monuments of Romanesque Art, The Art of Church Treasures in North-Western Europe.* London, 1954 (2nd ed., Chicago, 1967).

H. Swarzenski 1958
Swarzenski, Hanns. "The Song of the Three Worthies," *Bulletin* of the Museum of Fine Arts, Boston 56 (1958), pp. 30-49.

H. Swarzenski 1969
Swarzenski, Hanns. "A Medieval Treasury," *Apollo* 90 (1969), pp. 484-493.

De Tervarent 1950
De Tervarent, Guy. "Contribution à l'iconographie de Sainte Sophie et de ses trois filles," *Analecta Bollandiana*, 1950, pp. 419-423.

Thoby 1953
Thoby, Paul. *Les Croix limousines.* Paris, 1953.

Thompson 1933
Cennini, Cennino d'Andrea. *Il libro dell'arte* (Daniel V. Thompson, ed.) New Haven, 1933.

Toesca 1908
Toesca, Pietro. "Vetri italiani a oro con graffiti," *L'Arte* 11 (1908), pp. 247-261.

De Vaivre 1974
De Vaivre, Jean Bernard. "Le Décou héraldique de la cassette d'Aix-la-Chapelle," *Aachener Kunstblatter* 45 (1974), pp. 97-124.

Varty 1967
Varty, Kenneth. *Reynard the Fox.* Leicester, 1967.

Verdier 1956
Verdier, Philippe. "A Medallion of the Ara Coeli and the Netherlandish Enamels of the Fifteenth Century," *Journal of the Walters Art Gallery* 19-20 (1956-1957), pp. 8-37.

Verdier 1970
Verdier, Philippe. "La Grande Croix de L'Abbé Suger à Saint-Denis," *Cahiers de civilisation médiévales* 13 (1970), pp. 1-31.

Verdier 1974
Verdier, Philippe. "A Thirteenth-Century Monstrance in the Walters Art Gallery," *Gatherings in Honor of Dorothy Miner.* Baltimore, 1974, pp. 257-283.

Verdier 1975
Verdier, Philippe. "Emaux Mosans et Rheno-Mosans dans les collections des Etats-Unis," *Revue Belge d'archéologie et d'histoire de l'art* 44 (1975), pp. 1-84.

Verdier 1980
Verdier, Philippe. *Le Couronnement de la Vierge*. Montreal and Paris, 1980.

Verlet 1950
Verlet, Pierre. "Donation Larcade, Douze Disques de Limoges," *Bulletin des Musées de France* 15 (1950), pp. 6-7.

Vickers 1974
Vickers, Michael. "A Note on Glass Medallions in Oxford," *Journal of Glass Studies* 16 (1974), pp. 18-21.

Virginia 1966
European Art in the Virginia Museum of Fine Arts: A Catalogue. Richmond, 1966.

Volbach 1976
Volbach, W. F. *Elfenbeinarbeiten der Spätantike und des frühen Mittelalters*. Mainz, 1976.

Wallace 1924
Wallace Collection Catalogues, Objects of Art. London, 1924.

Warner 1912
Warner, George. *Queen Mary's Psalter*. London, 1912.

Washington 1981
Boyd, Susan, and Vikan, Gary. *Questions of Authenticity among the Arts of Byzantium*. Dumbarton Oaks, Washington, D.C., 1981.

Aus'm Weerth 1866
Aus'm Weerth, E. *Kunstdenkmäler des Christlichen Mittelalters in den Rheinlanden*. Leipzig, 1866, vol. 1, pt. 3.

Wentzel 1957
Wentzel, Hans. "Das Medaillen mit dem Hl. Theodor und die venezianischen Glaspasten im byzantinischen Stil," *Festschrift für Erich Meyer zum Sechizigsten Geburtstag*. Hamburg, 1957, pp. 50-67.

Wentzel 1963
Wentzel, Hans. "Zu dem enkolpion mit dem hl. Demetrios in Hamburg," *Jahrbuch der Hamburger Kunstsammlungen* 8 (1963), pp. 11-24.

Werner 1950
Werner, Joachim. *Die Langobardischen Fibeln aus Italien*. Berlin, 1950.

Werner 1966
Werner, Joachim. "Zu den donauländischen Beziehungen des alamannischen Gräberfeldes am alten Gotterbarmweg in Basel," *Helvetia Antiqua. Festschrift Emil Vogt*. Zurich, 1966, pp. 283-292.

Westwood 1868
Westwood, J. O. *Facsimiles of Miniatures and Ornaments in Anglo-Saxon and Irish Manuscripts*. London, 1868.

Willemin 1839
Willemin, N. X. *Monuments français inédits*. Vol. 1. Paris, 1839.

Woodward and Burnett 1892
Woodward, John, and Burnett, George. *A Treatise on Heraldry*. Edinburgh and London, 1892.

Young 1968
Young, Bonnie. "The Monkeys and the Peddler," *Metropolitan Museum of Art Bulletin* 26 (1968), pp. 441-454.

Zarnecki 1953
Zarnecki, George. *Later English Romanesque Sculpture 1140-1210*. London, 1953.

Zehender 1967
Zehender, G. "Die Siegburger Servatiusschatz," *Heimatbuch der Stadt Siegburg*. Vol. 2. Siegburg, 1967.

· INDEX ·